They Stood
ALONE!

They Stood
ALONE!

25
Men and Women
WHO MADE A DIFFERENCE

Sandra
McLeod
Humphrey

Prometheus Books

59 John Glenn Drive
Amherst, New York 14228-2119

Published 2011 by Prometheus Books

Cover image © 2011, Media Bakery
Cover design by Grace M. Conti-Zilsberger

Inquiries should be addressed to
Prometheus Books
59 John Glenn Drive
Amherst, New York 14228–2119
VOICE: 716–691–0133
FAX: 716–691–0137
WWW.PROMETHEUSBOOKS.COM

15   5 4

Library of Congress Cataloging-in-Publication Data

Humphrey, Sandra McLeod.
    They stood alone! : 25 men and women who made a difference / Sandra McLeod Humphrey.
        p. cm.
    Includes bibliographical references and index.
    ISBN 978–1–61614–485–2 (pbk. : alk. paper)
    ISBN 978–1–61614–486–9 (ebook)
    1. Biography—Juvenile literature. I. Title.

CT107.H79 2011
920.008—dc23
[B]   2011028697

Printed in the United States of America on acid-free paper

Heroes are ordinary people who accomplish
extraordinary things, and this book
is dedicated to all our heroes—
past, present, and future.

If a man does not keep pace with his companions, perhaps it is because he hears a different drummer.

Let him step to the music which he hears, however measured and far away.

—Henry David Thoreau (1817–1862)

contents

Contents

author's note

In the pages that follow you will have the opportunity to meet twenty-five extraordinary men and women.

Your choices for inclusion in this book might be different from mine, but I chose my individuals according to the following criteria:

- They were people of vision who saw life from a different or a new perspective.
- They were pioneers of a sort who were willing to question the conventional wisdom of their time.
- They had the courage to step out away from the crowd and take a risk.
- They believed in themselves and pursued their dreams in spite of societal opposition.
- And their revolutionary breakthroughs changed their world and ours.

It has been said that society frequently tends to honor its living conformists and its dead troublemakers. Those who have ever made a difference in any profession have generally followed their own hearts and proceeded independent of the opinions of others.

Author's Note

In every age there are courageous men and women who break with tradition to explore new ideas and challenge accepted truths.

So I invite you to have the courage to "step to the music" that only you can hear. And for those around you who hear a drumbeat that is foreign to you, they too must be allowed to step to the music they hear, even though it may sound strident and off-key to you.

The intent of this book is to inspire you to have your own dream and to follow your heart until you attain your dream.

So come along and join us as we meet twenty-five extraordinary men and women who made a difference!

Christopher Columbus

> "By prevailing over all obstacles and distractions, one may unfailingly arrive at his chosen goal or destination."
>
> —Christopher Columbus
> (1451–1506)

Imagine this: You have a theory that boldly contradicts something that everyone else believes to be true. You believe that you can reach the East by sailing west. You believe that your theory is correct, but if it proves to be wrong, it will bring you humiliation, financial ruin, and possibly death.

Your name is Christopher Columbus, and when most explorers are sailing parallel to the coastline on their expeditions, hugging the shore as closely as possible, you set out at a direct right angle to the shore, straight out into the unknown.

Columbus was born in Genoa, Italy, in 1451, the oldest of five children. He had little schooling, so he did not learn to read or write as a young boy.

But he did love to study maps and he did love the sea. He vowed that as soon as he was old enough, he would go to sea.

In his early teens he became a sailor and traveled to Greece and Portugal. While in Portugal, he studied the works and maps of ancient and modern geographers until he had taught himself all he could learn about navigation and mapmaking. The more he learned, the more convinced he became that the Atlantic Ocean was not populated by sea monsters and could be mastered.

He also became fascinated by Marco Polo's accounts of his journey to Asia and all the riches he had found there, but Columbus believed that the quickest and most direct route to the East was by sailing westward across the unknown waters that were called the Sea of Darkness.

His objective was not to prove the earth was round, for by the end of the fifteenth century, most educated people knew the earth was a sphere. His primary objective was to find a more direct route to the riches and rare spices of the East.

He asked King John II of Portugal to finance his expedition, but after consulting with his advisers, the king denied his request.

After King John II refused to finance his expedition, Columbus asked King Ferdinand and Queen Isabella of Spain. After several requests, they finally agreed to finance his voyage.

The Spanish rulers gave him three ships and paid for ninety crewmen and supplies. The ships were quite small by modern standards—no longer than a tennis court and less than thirty feet wide.

In 1492 Columbus and his crew set out, but once they were out of sight of land, his men grew fearful, so Columbus devised a false set of charts to show the crew so they wouldn't know how far they were actually going.[1]

In spite of the false set of charts, after thirty-four days at sea, his men became increasingly restless and began to threaten mutiny. Columbus convinced his crew to wait three more days, and the very next day they saw tree branches floating in the water and realized that land was close.

When they went ashore on October 12, 1492, Columbus proclaimed the land part of Spain and declared its inhabitants to be Spanish subjects.

Columbus was puzzled by the "easterners" who were dark-skinned and wore little clothing. He called them "Indians" because he thought he was in India, but they were not as Marco Polo had described them. Nor did he find any "cities of gold" or any "pagodas with golden roofs."

He named the island San Salvador and then explored the islands farther south still in search of gold (what is now Cuba and the surrounding islands).

In 1493 he left some of his crew in the New World to build a small colony while he and the rest of his crew returned to Spain. Unlike the trip over, the return trip was very rough with turbulent weather, but Columbus did manage to make it back to Spain.

The natives and parrots he brought back with him were living proof of his accomplishment. The widely published report of his voyage made him famous throughout Europe, secured for him the title of Admiral of the Ocean Sea, and led to three subsequent expeditions to the Caribbean.

Horses were introduced to the New World by Columbus on his second voyage.

Women were not on either the first or second voyage, but he was allowed to recruit one woman for every ten emigrants on the third voyage.

Even though Queen Isabella and King Ferdinand made him

Viceroy of any new lands he discovered and awarded him ten percent of any new wealth, his own administrative failings trying to govern the new territories led to disappointment and political obscurity in his final years.

Columbus was fifty-one years old and fairly sickly when he set out on his fourth and final voyage on May 11, 1502, with four aging ships and 150 men. Anxious to restore his good name, he was still determined to find the link between the Indies and the Indian Ocean. He arrived at Santo Domingo on June 29, 1502, but was refused entry into the harbor.

Besieged by storms and headwinds, the ships managed to work their way down the coast to what is now Panama. Some gold was found in this area, so the explorers set up a trading post. This venture was short-lived, however, as the native Indians grew unfriendly and forced the Spaniards to flee.

Exploration of these new regions was fraught with problems. Columbus was sick, the food was rotten, and the ships were worm-infested and leaking. And conditions only got worse. While anchored off Jamaica in 1504, supplies were running low, and the Jamaican Indians refused to sell him any more food. Consulting his almanac, Columbus noticed that a lunar eclipse was due a few days later. On the appointed day, he summoned the Jamaican leaders and warned them that he would blot out the moon that very evening if his demands for food were not promptly met. The Jamaicans only laughed at him until later that night when the eclipse began. As the moon disappeared before their eyes, they returned to Columbus in a state of terror, whereupon he agreed to stop his magic in exchange for food. The offer was accepted and the moon was "restored."[2]

After being stranded in Jamaica for more than a year, Columbus finally managed to make it home to Spain on

November 7, 1504, officially ending Columbus's last and most memorable voyage.

In spite of the fact that the Spanish crown retracted some of his privileges, Columbus was still a relatively rich man at the time of his death on May 20, 1506, and did not die a pauper as some people believe.

His discoveries changed the course of history. While he did not find the extraordinary cities of gold he had been seeking, his monumental exploits helped Spain enjoy a Golden Age until the end of the seventeenth century when England, France, and the Netherlands successfully challenged her power.

Columbus was the first European to navigate an Atlantic crossing from the Old World to the New World by setting course directly out into the ocean's vast, uncharted waters rather than hugging the shoreline.

During his voyages he traveled to the islands of the Caribbean Sea and explored the northeastern tip of South America and the eastern coast of Central America. He never did set foot on North American soil, but he did make it as far north as Cuba, only ninety miles from Florida.

He never abandoned the belief that he had reached Asia, and he went to his grave without ever realizing that he had explored and colonized two vast new continents.

Although the Vikings had set up temporary colonies in Greenland and Newfoundland around 1000 CE, the voyages of Columbus marked the beginning of the permanent European colonization of the Americas.

After five centuries, Columbus still remains one of the most famous, but also one of the most controversial, figures in history. He has been criticized for his exploitation of the native inhabitants and the destruction of their cultures, but he has also been praised as an explorer who played a key role in helping to spread European civilization across a significant portion of the earth. He has been described as one of the greatest mariners of all time, a visionary genius, a national hero, an unsuccessful entrepreneur, and a ruthless and greedy imperialist obsessed with his quest for gold and power.

But, regardless of how you feel about him, I think we can all agree that few events have altered the course of history as dramatically as his colonization of the Americas. He was a man of vision and courage in the face of uncertainty.

The Ultimate Renaissance Man

Leonardo **da Vinci**

"There are three class-
es of people. Those who
see; those who see
when they are shown;
those who do not see."
—Leonardo da Vinci
(1452–1519)

Imagine this: You are the son of a country gentleman, but instead of marrying your mother, your father marries someone of his own class. Because you are illegitimate, you are denied the educational privileges of children born within a marriage. This means that you receive the basic elementary education for boys of your day, but you are not allowed to attend any of the new universities.

Your name is Leonardo da Vinci, and although you receive very little formal education, you have such an inquring mind and so many talents in so many areas that you become known as one of the greatest intellects in the history of mankind. You are a man for all seasons: painter, sculptor, architect, musician, scientist, mathematician, engineer, inventor, and so much more!

Leonardo was born on April 15, 1452, the son of a peasant mother, Caterina, and a country gentleman, Ser Piero. His father, Ser Piero, was a lawyer and a leading citizen of Vinci, Italy, and instead of marrying Caterina, he married a woman of his own class.

By the time Leonardo was five, his mother had married someone of her own class, and Leonardo was living with his father and stepmother at his grandfather's house near the village of Vinci, twenty miles from Florence.

While growing up he was especially close to his young uncle Francesco, and it was probably with Francesco that Leonardo explored the countryside and began his lifelong fascination with nature.

Since Leonardo was illegitimate, he was denied the privileges of children born within a marriage. He received the basic elementary education for boys of his day (reading, writing, and arithmetic), but did not attend one of the new universities.

Instead, his "university" was the workshop of the famous Florentine artist Andrea del Verrocchio who took him on as a fifteen-year-old apprentice and fostered his talents. It has been suggested that Leonardo may have posed for Verrocchio's bronze sculpture of *David*.

After Leonardo had been studying with Verrocchio for some time, he helped paint a picture of St. John baptizing Jesus. Verrocchio had already finished most of the painting, but Leonardo painted one of the angels and completed the background. It is said that when Verrocchio saw Leonardo's angel, he was so struck by how much finer it was than anything else in the painting that he never picked up a paintbrush again.[3]

When Leonardo was twenty, he was accepted into the

painters' guild but began projects only to abandon them. He enjoyed sketching and planning the composition of the picture, but he did not particularly enjoy the long and meticulous process of painting itself, so many of his projects were left unfinished. Only seventeen of his paintings survive.

At about age thirty, he headed north to Milan. The Duchy of Milan was ruled by Duke Ludovico Sforza who was called the Moor after the Arabs of North Africa because of his dark complexion.

After the Moor became Leonardo's patron, Leonardo was kept busy doing whatever his patron wanted, anything from designing a heating system for the duchess's bath to painting a portrait of the Moor's favorite lady.

The world saw Leonardo as courtly and charming, but at heart he was a solitary man who enjoyed being alone. In the peace of his aloneness he could imagine, create, and dream.

He began writing in his famous notebooks when he was about thirty, and over the years, he filled thousands of pages with the outpourings of his amazing mind. In 1994, Bill Gates, chairman of the Microsoft Corporation, bought one of these notebooks for $30 million.[4]

His notebooks included drafts of letters, sketches for future paintings, plans for inventions, moral observations, designs for weapons, drawings of anatomy, and observations of nature. On one page, for example, you can find geometry problems, a plan for building canals, and the note, "Tuesday: bread, meat, wine, fruit, vegetables, salad."[5]

"I question" were the words he wrote most frequently in his notebooks. He asked such questions as: What causes tickling? Why are stars invisible during the day? What would it be like to walk on water? Would a fly make a different sound if you put honey on its wings?[6]

To Leonardo the key to everything was *saper vedere*—"knowing how to see." He wanted to be like a camera—what he referred to as "becoming like a mirror."[7]

The fact that he wrote everything in a peculiar backward script, going from right to left, so that a mirror is necessary to read it has led to the myth that he wrote that way to keep his notebooks safe from prying eyes. A much more likely explanation, however, is that since he was left-handed, he found it much easier to write that way. When he *really* wanted to keep something secret, he wrote in code.

Perhaps the most impressive drawings in his notebooks are those that show his careful study of anatomy. Not only did he study the human body as an artist, but he also approached anatomy as a scientist. Over a period of twenty-five years he dissected some thirty corpses, making almost two hundred painstaking drawings of them. He also dissected bears, cows, monkeys, birds, and frogs, comparing their structures to those of humans.

Much of what Leonardo drew did not technically get invented for centuries: contact lenses, cars, bicycles, expressways, airplanes, helicopters, prefabricated houses, burglarproof locks, automatic door closers, submarines, life preservers, steam engines, and tanks.

In those days people answered questions by looking them up in the Bible or in the writings of the ancient Greeks, but Leonardo believed that people who did this were using their memories, not their minds. Instead, he followed what today we call the scientific method.

First, he observed things carefully, like the movement of water or the flight of birds. That led him to ask questions such as why does a pot lid jump up and down when water starts to boil? Then, in attempting to explain what he observed, he made a hypothesis which he then had to prove. Often he wasn't satisfied until he had measured it, so he invented all sorts of devices to measure humidity, altitude, distance traveled, angle of inclination, speed of wind and water, and intensity of light.

He was also a mechanical genius and perhaps the most visionary man of all time. Few individuals in the history of engineering have designed so many revolutionary devices that actually worked. Among his many inventions were an underwater diving apparatus, an automatic paper feeder for a printing press, one of the world's first air-cooling systems, a door that closed automatically, a posthole digger, a submarine, pliers, and a spring-powered car.

He loved animals so much that he eventually became a vegetarian and was said to buy caged birds at markets just to set them free. And yet this gentle man invented some fearsome war machines: three different models of machine guns, grenades that threw shrapnel, a very modern-looking bomb, and a steam-powered gun.

As an inventor, he is probably most famous for having tried to build a flying machine. He analyzed the flight patterns of birds and bats, studied the anatomy of their wings, and observed air currents.

He also sketched the pattern of a leaf drifting to earth, and under it showed a man on a winglike glider. If he had only worked along these lines instead of trying to imitate the flapping motion of birds, he might have been the first man to fly.

Around 1516 or 1517 the King of France, Francis I, offered him the title Premier Painter and Engineer and Architect of the King. He was well paid, he was given a charming manor house, and all the king expected in return was Leonardo's conversation.

Leonardo brought with him his notebooks and three paintings, one of which was called *La Gioconda* which we know as the *Mona Lisa*, probably the most famous painting in the world.

It is said that Leonardo died on May 2, 1519, at age sixty-seven with the King of France at his bedside.

Leonardo da Vinci has been called the ultimate Renaissance man—an all-around genius whose contributions to the arts and sciences changed the world.

A New and Revolutionary View of the Cosmos

Nicolaus **Copernicus**

"To know that we know what we know, and to know that we do not know what we do not know, that is true knowledge."

—Nicolaus Copernicus (1473–1543)

Imagine this: For centuries everyone has believed that the sun and all the planets revolve around the earth. But you have studied all the old books and by studying astronomy and the heavens, you have concluded that the sun, not the earth, is the center of the solar system and that the earth and all the other planets revolve around the sun. Your theory is so radical that you are hesitant to even tell others about it.

Your name is Nicolaus Copernicus, and this is the very situation in which you find yourself in the sixteenth century. Although initially your beliefs are denounced and ridiculed, your observations are eventually proven to be correct, and you come to be called the founding father of modern astronomy.

Copernicus was born on February 11, 1473, in Torun, Poland, the youngest of four children. His family was relatively wealthy, but his father died when Copernicus was ten years old, and his mother's brother stepped in to help the family.

In the fifteenth century students learned by memorization and repetition, and schools did not emphasize imagination or learning to think for oneself.

Copernicus and his brother attended the University of Krakow in Poland while his two sisters were not offered an education beyond grammar school because girls at that time did not attend college.

At the University of Krakow he mastered mathematics, optics, and perspective. He then continued his study of both astrology and astronomy at the University of Bologna in Italy where he also studied canon law to prepare himself for the career in the church he was expected to pursue in his uncle's footsteps. After Bologna, he attended the University of Padua, where he concentrated on medicine.

When he finished his education, he was thirty years old and returned to Poland where he served his uncle as personal physician and secretary for the next several years.

When his day's duties were done, he spent his nights studying the heavens, and he noticed things that did not make sense.

The astronomy books he had studied were written over a thousand years earlier, mostly by ancient Greek philosophers and scientists.

Claudius Ptolemy, a Greek scientist and mathematician in the second century CE, was one of the authorities Copernicus had studied, and Ptolemy believed the earth stayed motionless in the center of the universe while all the other planets and the sun revolved around it.

But Copernicus did not agree. He believed in a cosmology

much different from that which had been universally accepted for almost a millennium and a half.

In Copernicus's time there were two different branches of science that dealt with the universe: astronomy (which used mathematical models to predict celestial motions) and cosmology (which dealt with the physical structure of the universe).

Ptolemy was an astronomer, Aristotle was a cosmologist, and Copernicus was a mathematical astronomer.

The more Copernicus studied lunar and solar eclipses and the passage of planets in front of certain stars, the more convinced he became that Ptolemy's solar model was wrong.

The answer that revealed itself from all of his calculations was revolutionary. It went so much against what people believed that he hesitated to tell anyone about it.

His theory transferred the earth from its special place at the center of the universe. It made earth just another planet, like Mars or Mercury, circling a common center. And that center was the sun.

And that wasn't the only revolutionary thing about Copernicus's theory. In the old, accepted system, the earth stood still as the universe whirled around it. Day and night happened because the sun circled the earth every twenty-four hours. The only way to explain day and night under Copernicus's theory was for the earth to rotate while the sun stood still.

Copernicus also determined the order the planets were in and approximately how far away from the sun they were. This proper order and spacing of the planets was something Ptolemy's model was unable to do.

Copernicus worked on his theory his entire life. He studied astronomy in his spare time and was one of the few medieval or Renaissance astronomers who did not make his living as an astrologer. In fact, Copernicus did not even believe much in astrology.

After his uncle died, Copernicus took up his religious duties as a canon, but his heart was really in his astronomy. He knew that for such a revolutionary theory to be accepted, he would have to offer mathematical details.

Working almost entirely on his own, he assembled the evidence to show that his ideas were plausible even though they could not be fully proven with the scientific instruments then available.

His innovative ideas also meant that the lengths of years and months could be calculated more precisely than ever before.

He worked on a book that not only proposed his theory but also showed how it worked. It was a book only a mathematician could read and understand completely.

He probably began writing his book explaining his heliocentric theory (that the sun was the center of the universe and that all heavenly bodies, including the earth, revolved around it) around 1515 and finished most of the writing around 1530, but he continued to revise his work for years afterward.

His findings went against the teachings of Aristotle and Ptolemy and the classical astronomical view of a universe that centered around a stationary earth that people had believed for 1,400 years.

It took courage for Copernicus to challenge an idea that had been around for so long, and people did not like what he told them. They wanted to go on believing that the earth was the center of the universe. If his theory were correct, then the church was wrong, and many Catholic clergymen refused to believe that the church was wrong.

In 1543 he published his astronomical findings in his book *On the Revolution of the Heavenly Spheres* which is often regarded as the starting point of modern astronomy and the defining epiphany that began the scientific revolution.

That same year he also suffered a stroke which left his right side paralyzed. By the time he received a copy of his published book, he was barely alive and he saw his completed work on the day he died, May 24, 1543.

Although Copernicus had spent his professional career as a minor official in the Roman Catholic Church, it was his theories about astronomy he had written down in his book that made up his real life's work. His great passion was the stars, and he spent his entire life developing and refining a view of the universe that was in opposition to the established beliefs of his day.

He never knew what a stir his ideas would create in the years to come or how they would change the course of astronomy forever.

Humans were no longer the center of the universe or even the center of attraction. Copernicus's ideas changed the way people thought about the world and themselves. His ideas changed everything.

After his death, his remains rested in an unmarked grave beneath the floor of the cathedral in Frombork, Poland, for more than 450 years.

Although initially his beliefs were denounced and ridiculed, scientists with more advanced instruments and telescopes have now proven that the earth does indeed revolve around the sun. Many of our modern advances in science would not have been possible without the heliocentric theory of Copernicus which is why he is considered to be the founding father of modern astronomy.

His life and his work inspire us to embrace new concepts and realities in our lives, even if they undermine everything that we have always thought to be true.

It wasn't until May 22, 2010, that the astronomer whose findings had been condemned by the Roman Catholic Church as heretical, was reburied by Polish priests as a hero in the cathedral in Frombork. His tombstone identifies him as the founder of the heliocentric theory and is decorated with a model of the solar system, a golden sun encircled by six of the planets.[8]

The Father of Modern Science

"The earth does move."

—Galileo Galilei
(1564–1642)

Imagine this: You believe that Copernicus was right and that the earth *does* revolve around the sun, and you set out to prove it at the risk of displeasing the church and many of those in authority.

Your name is Galileo Galilei, and you take great risks to prove that Copernicus's heliocentric theory is correct. Pope Paul V objects to all of your findings which are contrary to what the church believes and warns you to stop teaching the Copernican cosmology. You, however, are dedicated to searching for the truth, and your belief that you prove a theory by doing experiments ushers in the scientific revolution.

Galileo was born in Pisa, Italy, in 1564, the eldest of seven children of the Galilei family, an old and noble Florentine line that had fallen on hard times.

His mother was well educated, which was unusual for women of her day. And his father was a respected musician and an outspoken, uncompromising man who defended his ideas regardless of whom he challenged or offended. From an early age, Galileo was taught by his father to think for himself and to question authority.

His family moved from Pisa to Florence, a cultural center, where Galileo studied Latin, Greek, mathematics, religion, music, and painting. His constant questioning while still a student earned him the nickname "the Wrangler."

At seventeen he enrolled as a medical student at the University of Pisa, and his financially strained family hoped he would become a rich doctor.

While in the Cathedral of Pisa three years later, his attention was caught by a big lamp hanging from the cathedral ceiling that was swaying in a draft. He timed its movements with the beat of his pulse and discovered that each swing of the lamp, no matter how great or small, took the same amount of time. Twenty-year old Galileo had recognized a simple truth, the law of the pendulum.[9] He then went on to design the pendulum clock that advanced the study of physics and astronomy.

He gave up the study of medicine because he was more interested in matter, energy, motion, and force—the science of physics. After four years he had to leave the university without graduating because his family had become too poor to continue his education.

Over the next several years Galileo mastered mathematics and physics with the help of a family friend, Ostilio Ricci, a professor of mathematics.

His reputation was growing, and even though he had not been able to graduate from the University of Pisa, he returned there in 1589 as a professor of mathematics. He quickly made enemies by challenging a nearly two-thousand-year-old theory of Aristotle's.

Aristotle believed that if two different weights were dropped from the same height, the heavier would hit the ground first. Galileo tested this by dropping several weights from the Leaning Tower of Pisa. They fell at the same speed, and he observed that the longer an object falls, the faster it falls. Those observations later helped Newton develop his law of universal gravity. But those who were loyal followers of Aristotle refused to believe their eyes, and they forced Galileo out of the university.

Thanks to Galileo's reputation and his influential friends, he became a professor at the University of Padua. There he continued to question long-held beliefs, and his experiments drew students from all over Europe to the University of Padua.

When he built a telescope which allowed him to see an object thirty-three times larger than its actual size, he began to study the stars. But many people refused to believe his astronomical findings because they were in conflict with the ancient teachings.

Designing his own, improved telescope, he was the first to recognize that the Milky Way consists of millions of stars, and in 1610 he discovered sunspots and the moons of Jupiter.

One night in 1610 when he was studying Jupiter, he observed that Jupiter had four moons of its own which revolved around the planet, and Galileo began to think that there was some truth to the Copernican belief that the earth was not the center of the universe.

In 1610 Galileo published a small book, *The Starry*

Messenger, in which he described his observations, and he began to make and sell his telescopes, so that people could verify his observations for themselves. But many people refused to use his telescope, preferring to cling to their old beliefs.

To amuse his friends, he built a microscope for looking at insects while he continued to study the heavens.

And the more he studied them, the more certain he was that Copernicus was right and that the sun did stand still while the planets and other heavenly bodies traveled around it.

Galileo's heavenly explorations met with powerful resistance because they were in opposition to the beliefs long held by the Catholic Church and ancient scholars.

Pope Paul V continued to object to all of Galileo's findings which disputed what the church believed, and in 1616 he officially denounced the Copernican theory and instructed Galileo to stop teaching his Copernican cosmology. Galileo was stunned and was more determined than ever to prove that Copernicus was right.

In 1626 a group of powerful churchmen and professors convinced Galileo to talk about his findings as only a theory, a possibility.

But by 1632 he could no longer deny what he knew was the truth. He published *Dialogue*—his most famous work—that supported the work of Copernicus and ridiculed the followers of Aristotle.

The book was a best-seller, but since the book argued that the church was wrong, Pope Urban VIII banned the book.

The Pope then ordered the sixty-eight-year-old ailing Galileo to Rome to appear before the Holy Office of the Inquisition where he was accused of upholding the Copernican theory of the universe after being warned not to.

Finally, too sick and exhausted to protest any more, Galileo announced on his knees that Copernicus was wrong and that he was wrong to have publicly promoted Copernicus's theory.

He signed a paper attesting to his errors and was confined to his house in Arcetri, outside Florence, away from places of learning, for the rest of his life.

Four years later in 1637 and still imprisoned in his house, Galileo became totally blinded by an infection. After he became blind, his secretary and assistant Vincenzio Vivani helped him with his writing and wrote his letters for him.

The following year Galileo published his papers about force and motion that made it possible for Sir Isaac Newton, an English mathematician, to discover the laws of gravity and motion twenty-seven years later.

When Galileo died in 1642 at age seventy-two, he was still considered guilty of spreading beliefs that were contrary to church teachings, and Pope Urban VIII never forgave him for his disobedience. Pope Urban was so angry that he refused to allow a statue of Galileo to be erected in front of the Church of Santa Croce in Florence where Galileo was buried.

It was not until 1992, after a thirteen-year debate over the conflict between science and faith, that Pope John Paul II formally closed the Catholic Church's case against Galileo and acknowledged the truth of Galileo's arguments and those of Copernicus.

In his uncompromising search for the truth, Galileo ushered in the scientific revolution and was one of the first scientists to try to prove a theory by doing experiments.

Called the father of modern science, he was truly a man who changed the world. He believed the secrets of the universe would be revealed through careful observation. He constructed the thermoscope to measure heat, the microscope to magnify insects, and a telescope to see the stars. And, most important, he demonstrated that the Polish astronomer Copernicus was right: The earth is *not* the center of the universe.

By changing the way people saw the galaxy, Galileo also changed the way they saw themselves and their place in the universe.

Galileo took the full force of the punishment for being different in a time that demanded conformity.

Scientist and Mathematician Extraordinaire

Isaac **Newton**

"Errors are not in the art but in the artificers."
—Isaac Newton
(1642–1727)

Imagine this: It's the summer of 1666, you are twenty-two years old, and you are sitting beneath a tree in your mother's orchard.

You have already been trying to understand what keeps the moon in its orbit around the earth and the planets in their courses around the sun, but after an apple falls on your head, you begin to search seriously for the answers to your questions.

Your name is Isaac Newton, and your achievements in physics and mathematics will be the basis of physics and mathematics for the next three hundred years. You are considered by many to be one of the greatest scientists of all time.

Newton was born prematurely just after midnight on

They Stood Alone!

Christmas Day 1642 (the same year that Galileo died) in the manor house of Woolsthorpe in Lincolnshire, England, and was not expected to survive. His father, a fairly prosperous farmer, had died three months earlier, leaving Isaac's mother, Hannah, to raise the tiny boy on her own.

His mother remarried when he was three years old, a marriage of convenience, so that she could provide for her son. Her new husband, a wealthy clergyman, insisted that Newton remain with his maternal grandmother at Woolsthorpe Manor, so that Hannah could look after her new family.

Newton's childhood was a lonely time. He made few friends and kept to himself, often spending the day in his room making models, kites, sundials, and little mechanical devices.

Before long, he became well known in the district for his creations, and local people were amazed by his skill at constructing exact replicas of carts and wheeled machines.

When he was ten, his stepfather died and his mother returned to live at the manor with her three children from her second marriage.

Newton was considered an average student by his teachers and antisocial by his classmates. He admitted later that he ignored his studies and spent most of his time making models and carrying out his own experiments.

When provoked by a school bully much larger than himself who also happened to be first academically, Newton fought back and ended up winning the fight. After his victory, he decided that if he could beat the bully physically, maybe he was also his match academically, and he began to pay more attention to his studies. He became an intellectual leader, gaining the respect of his teachers and his classmates. Before the fight, he was near the bottom of his class. After the fight, he worked his way up to becoming the top student at his school.[10]

In 1661, the eighteen-year old Newton was admitted to the prestigious Cambridge University. His mother refused to pay his tuition because she wanted him back home to run the family farm, so he earned his keep by cleaning the rooms of the paying students, serving meals, and doing menial jobs.

At Cambridge he read everything he could by the great mathematicians, scientists, and philosophers of the time and graduated in 1664. He remained at Cambridge after graduation to pursue graduate study.

In 1664 he began his experiments with light and discovered that when white light is shone through a prism, it splits into a rainbow which he called the spectrum, the light ranging from violet at the top to red at the bottom.

Once an experiment was devised, he repeated it many times in order to eliminate errors or any possibility of chance. He then kept impeccable records of his findings.

When The Great Plague broke out in London in 1665, Cambridge University was forced to close its doors for a year, and twenty-three-year-old Newton returned home for that year.

He later called 1666 his "Miraculous Year" because it was there in the solitude of the family's countryside manor that he began to make incredible breakthroughs in mathematics and physics including the answer to a problem that had eluded the most gifted mathematicians for years—the binomial theorem. He did his greatest thinking during those eighteen months and he worked harder than ever.

It was also in 1666 at Wolsthorpe where the famous legend of Newton and the apple was born. While he was napping under a tree, an apple fell on his head and he awoke with a jolt.

According to the legend, he wondered why the apple always fell down and concluded that the apple falling and the moon orbiting were governed by the same force: gravity—or what Newton later referred to as the law of universal gravitation.[11]

Soon after that he began to work on what was to be the greatest development in the history of mathematics—calculus.

In 1667 he was made a fellow at Trinity College and, in spite of living in the middle of a busy university, he led a solitary life. He usually ate in his own room, and when he did join the other professors in the college dining room, he was often lost in thought and sometimes forgot to eat.

Newton's ability to concentrate was extraordinary, and according to one legend, he dismounted on his way home from town one day and walked his horse by its bridle so it could rest. As always, his mind wandered. Perhaps he was thinking about the four-wheel carriage he'd just built or the system of shorthand he'd created, or maybe he was just watching the sunlight on the grass and wondering what made the grass green. Miles and hours later he arrived home not even aware that the horse had long ago slipped out of its bridle, and he had walked the whole way back, alone.[12]

Newton was also very untidy, rarely bothering to change his clothes or fasten his shoes or comb his long hair. He seldom got any exercise either because he felt any time away from his studies was time lost.

He was required to give one lecture a week, but very few people attended his lectures because few understood them. Sometimes there was no one there at all and he read to the walls.

The work Newton began during the "Miraculous Year" would be the basis of mathematics and physics for the next three hundred years.

Newton's laws of motion explain how forces act upon objects, whether moving or stationary. By applying these laws to any mechanical system, it's possible to predict the effect a force will have on an object.

He also worked out a theory of gravity to explain how the planets travel in their orbits around the sun. The same theory also explains why we remain held firmly to earth and do not all float off into space.

His book *Principia Mathematica*, which he wrote in only eighteen months, was published in 1687 and contained what became known as Newton's laws of motion. This is considered by many to be the greatest scientific work ever produced.

In 1705 he was knighted by Queen Anne for his great work in both science and public service, the first scientist ever to be honored in this way.

Sir Isaac Newton died a painful death on March 20, 1727, at age eighty-four from gout, lung inflammation, and kidney stones. He was buried among Britain's kings and queens in London's Westminster Abbey, the first scientist to be so honored.

Today, more than 350 years after his birth, scientists from around the world still use the very same principles and ideas that were first laid down by his *Principia* in 1687.

Newton created an entirely new approach to science and an original way of solving many of its most fundamental problems. He once explained that when he was faced with a problem, he kept it in his mind until he solved it. He often went without food or sleep until he was satisfied with his answer.

Today, Newton's laws of motion are used in all areas of science such as designing cars, planning the course of a spaceship, and building aircraft engines. And the calculations needed to successfully complete the 500,000-mile round-trip to the moon are based on his law of universal gravity.

Without his revolutionary method of mathematical calculation—calculus—no major scientific discovery such as Einstein's theory of relativity would have been possible.

Isaac Newton was indisputably one of the greatest scientists in history. The discoverer of the fundamental laws of physics and the inventor of calculus, his achievements marked the culmination of the movement that brought modern science into being.

He once said, "If I have seen further than most men, it is by standing on the shoulders of giants."[13] His "giants" included such great men as Copernicus, Kepler, Galileo, and Descartes.

Suffragist and Reformer

Elizabeth Cady Stanton

" We hold these truths to be self-evident: that all men and women are created equal."
—Elizabeth Cady Stanton (1815–1902)

Imagine this: It's the early nineteenth century and women have few legal rights. Married women can not own property and their wages belong to their husbands. Women have no right of inheritance, and women have no right to the guardianship of their children. You know the laws are unfair, but as a young woman yourself, what can you do?

Your name is Elizabeth Cady Stanton, and you believe that the right to vote is the key to women's equality. You spend your life fighting for women's rights, and you are later given credit by many for being the architect and founder of the Women's Rights Movement itself.

Elizabeth was born November 12, 1815, in Johnstown, New York, one of six children of Margaret Livingston and Daniel Cady, the town's most prominent citizens. Her father was a judge and had served in the New York state legislature in Albany.

Elizabeth disliked her restrictive clothing: the long skirts; the red stockings; the heavy, red, flannel dresses with starched ruffles at the throat that scratched her skin; and the black aprons.

Indeed, she disliked restriction of any kind, and Elizabeth and her younger sister Margaret took a vow together to defy parental authority and to act as they chose. They were happy with their self-government and congratulated themselves, for they believed that had they obeyed all the orders and rules laid down for their guidance, they would have been "as embalmed mummies."[14]

Growing up she spent a lot of time in her father's law office where she saw how few legal rights women had. Married women could not own property and their wages belonged to their husbands; women had no right of inheritance, and they had no right to the guardianship of their children. A husband could apprentice their offspring without the mother's consent, and he could even appoint another guardian to raise them in the event of his death.

She was so disturbed by the unfairness of the laws that she once threatened to get scissors and cut the offending laws from the law books.

When her father realized her intent, he explained to her how laws were proposed and passed and told her the only way to get rid of old laws was to pass new ones.

As bright and feisty as his daughter Elizabeth was, her father was much more interested in his last-surviving son Eleazar whom he hoped would also become a judge. When

Eleazar was killed in an accident right after his graduation from Union College, her father was devastated.

While her father grieved for his lost son, Elizabeth did her best to be the son her father wanted. She was determined to be all that her brother had been, and to do that she believed that she had to be both educated and courageous.

She asked the Presbyterian minister next door to teach her Greek—something usually taught only to boys—and she learned to ride a horse.

She fought for and won the best possible education available to a young woman in America. She studied Greek and math and earned many academic prizes. And on horseback she could jump any fence without fear.

Despite all her accomplishments, however, her father still lamented the death of Eleazar, and the best he could do was to tell her, "Ah, you should have been a boy!"

Since colleges did not accept women, she enrolled in the Troy Female Seminary. It was the best education available to a young woman, but she knew that there was a great difference between a young men's college and even the most advanced female seminary.

After graduating from the Troy Female Seminary in 1833, she spent time in Peterboro, New York, with her cousin Gerrit Smith. While at the Smith home she was introduced to a young, escaped slave girl named Harriet who was on her way to Canada. After hearing Harriet's story, Elizabeth became a confirmed abolitionist herself.

At Peterboro she learned about racial injustice and was in constant contact with reformers of all kinds: abolitionists, temperance workers, philanthropists, and religious reformers. She felt drawn to the idea of an active life with purpose, a life that mattered.

She also felt drawn to another of Gerrit Smith's guests, Henry B. Stanton, ten years her senior. He was an abolitionist hero, and she joined him at antislavery conventions.

In spite of her father's objections, she married Stanton in 1840 in a service with only a few friends present. Believing that she and Henry would be equal partners, she insisted that the word "obey" be dropped from her marriage vows.[15]

They both became involved in the abolitionist cause, but Elizabeth was angered to find that many abolitionists believed that only men should represent the cause at conventions.

She and her friend, Lucretia Mott, decided to hold a convention of their own where they would debate another burning issue, that of equal rights for women.

During the eight years it took them to organize the convention, Elizabeth was busy raising her three boys virtually by herself while her husband traveled.

The first Women's Rights Convention took place on July 19, 1848, at Seneca Falls, New York, and three hundred people gathered to hear the arguments. Elizabeth gave the first speech which shocked many people who thought it was "unladylike" for a woman to address a crowd.

She proclaimed that it was the duty of the women of this country to win the right to vote. Her speech, the "Declaration of Rights and Sentiments," called for freedom and equality for women, and she argued that women could only attain their "inalienable rights" by winning the right to vote. Her controversial, radical ideas sparked a fight that would last for seventy-two years—the struggle for women's suffrage in America.

The Declaration of Sentiments was modeled after the United States Declaration of Independence. The first sentence differed by only two words: "*and women.*"

The two-day Seneca Falls convention marked the birth of

the Women's Rights Movement, and the United States would never be the same again.

When Susan Brownell Anthony, a young Quaker woman in Massachusetts, heard about the convention, she knew that she had to meet Elizabeth.

Elizabeth and Susan became a team. Elizabeth, now the mother of six, found traveling hard, so she wrote the speeches and Susan delivered them.

Together, they set out to win property rights for married women who were not allowed to own property themselves, and in 1860, New York State passed a law allowing married women control over the money they earned and anything they inherited.

But this was only the beginning. Now Elizabeth and Susan were determined to secure for women the right to vote. The two women launched a speaking tour and gathered thousands of signatures on petitions; Elizabeth wrote pamphlets that Susan sold to raise money; they started a newspaper called *The Revolution*; and they published books on the history of the Women's Rights Movement.

In her eighties Elizabeth developed cataracts with progressive blindness, but she nevertheless continued to work for suffrage until the very end of her life. On October 25, 1902, she wrote a letter to President Theodore Roosevelt urging the complete emancipation of thirty-six million women just as Lincoln had emancipated the slaves.

It was the last of her letters. On October 26, 1902, just a few weeks short of her eighty-seventh birthday, Elizabeth Cady Stanton died.

She had been involved in a lifelong struggle to obtain equality for women. It would take another seventy-two years after the first Women's Rights Convention for women to get the vote, and Elizabeth herself was never able to vote.

Finally on August 26, 1920, the United States passed the Nineteenth Amendment to the Constitution granting all women the right to vote. Without the work of Elizabeth Cady Stanton and Susan B. Anthony, women would not have received the right to vote as soon as they did.

Elizabeth Cady Stanton had succeeded in doing just what her father had said—replacing an old law with a new law.

"Simplicity, Simplicity, Simplicity!"

Henry David **Thoreau**

"If a man does not keep pace with his companions, perhaps it is because he hears a different drummer."

—Henry David Thoreau
(1817–1862)

Imagine this: Although you are Harvard educated, you decide at the age of twenty-seven, to build a small house with your own hands in the woods where you can study nature and not get caught up in the materialistic pressures of the world around you. Your aim is not to escape civilization but to simplify it. At the time, people criticize your simple way of life, but you have always been an independent thinker, and you continue to live your own life the way you want to.

Your name is Henry David Thoreau, and you champion the independence of the human spirit over materialism and social conformity. Through your writings, you become one of the most influential figures in American thought and literature.

Thoreau was born July 12, 1817, at his grandmother's unpainted farmhouse near Concord, Massachusetts, the third of four children. His father, following the family tradition, was a shopkeeper, but he had failed in business and by the time Thoreau was born, the family was very poor even by the standards of 1817.

Thoreau was baptized David Henry Thoreau and was so called until he chose to reverse his given names when he was twenty as an expression of his independence.

While Thoreau's father was quiet and studious, his mother was friendly, outgoing, and had a generous heart. Despite her own family's financial problems, she always found a way to help those poorer than herself and everyone was welcome in her home. She was also known to speak her mind on the social and political issues of the day, particularly on such subjects as slavery to which she was strongly opposed.

Thoreau enjoyed growing up in Concord where he could spend his time outdoors enjoying nature. He prepared for Harvard at the Concord Academy which offered courses in Latin, Greek, and French, and he entered Harvard at sixteen where he was primarily interested in the classics.

His years at Harvard opened him to a world of books, and he was deeply influenced by writers such as Thomas Carlyle and Ralph Waldo Emerson. Thoreau and Emerson became good friends, and it was probably Emerson who suggested that Thoreau keep a journal which became the heart of his work.

He graduated from Harvard in 1837 and was not a particularly outstanding student because of his independent ways. After his graduation, he returned to Concord and did begin keeping a journal to record his thoughts and ideas.

In the fall of 1838 he and his brother John opened a private school of their own. There would be no physical punishment, which was quite commonplace back then, and their students would learn by doing.

Thoreau offered languages and science and John taught English and mathematics. There were always plenty of field trips, which included trips to the local businesses, such as the newspaper and the gunsmith shop, as well as the usual nature trips.

The school's reputation was so high that there was usually a waiting list, but in 1841 Thoreau had to close the school when his brother became ill and could no longer teach.

Thoreau had always been interested in living a simple life, away from the intense pressures of a competitive society. Above all, he wanted to live his own kind of life. He believed that a person might live differently from his neighbors because he heard a "different drummer." If so, "let him step to the music which he hears," Thoreau wrote, "however measured or far away."

There was a pond near Concord named Walden, and this was one of his favorite places to just sit and think. In 1845 when he was in his late twenties, he built a little house on one of Walden's shores, a place where he could be alone. The house was very simple: it had one room, one table, one bed, and three chairs.

To Thoreau, nature was like a living being, and he wanted to do more than just enjoy its beauty. He wanted to get so close to it that he became one with it.

One entire morning he lay on his stomach and watched a war between red and black ants. And, once, a mouse ran up his sleeve as he sat outside eating, and he fed it some cheese. Then he watched while it nibbled and cleaned its face with its paws.

Thoreau had another important reason for going to live at Walden. He wanted to prove something to himself and to other people as well that someone could live very, very simply.

He was sure that most people were not happy but lived lives of "quiet desperation." He felt that people worked hard to own things and then when they finally did, they were still not satisfied. And then taking care of the things they had earned was often more trouble than it was worth. He once said, "It's never clear if the man owns the house or the house owns the man."

That's why Thoreau's house was simple and his food was plain. Living so simply left him free to do what he really wanted to do: to see and learn and think and write.

One of his mottos was, "simplicity, simplicity, simplicity!" When people traveled to California to find gold, he wrote, "Look for it within yourself."

And when someone praised Harvard College for teaching "all the branches of knowledge," he simply answered, "Yes, all the *branches* but none of the *roots*."

New clothes were not important to him, and one of his favorite expressions was, "Sell your clothes and keep your thoughts."

Once, while still living at Walden, he was even jailed briefly for refusing to pay a tax. At the time, the United States was waging what Thoreau felt was an unjust war against Mexico. This, along with his opposition to slavery, led him to refuse to support the government with his tax money.

He also hated how Native Americans were being treated by the white man, and he called the popular practice of removing Indians from their lands our very own Holocaust.

In 1849 he published his first book, *A Week on the Concord and Merrimack Rivers*, and the same year he also published his most famous short essay, "Civil Disobedience."

His most famous book, *Walden,* was published in 1854 and tells why he went to Walden, what he did there, and what he believed life's purposes to be. Although *Walden* wasn't recognized as a masterpiece and one of the great American classics of nonfiction until after his death, it has never gone out of print and it has appeared in more than 150 different editions, often selling in the hundreds of thousands of copies.

Despite the emphasis in *Walden* on solitude, Thoreau was not a hermit but a man deeply involved with family, friends, and the world around him.

He had many friends including the novelist Nathaniel Hawthorne and the philosopher Ralph Waldo Emerson. Friends were important to him, and he once wrote, "Friends are kind to each other's dreams."

He left his Walden house after two years because his life had become too routine. He felt he had other lives to live and had spent enough time on that one.[16]

In his early forties, his health began to fail, and while he could still move about, he took one final walk to Walden by the quiet water that he loved.

When he died on May 6, 1862, at age forty-four from tuberculosis, Concord lost its most distinguished son, and the nation lost a man and writer unique in any age.

But that was not the end of his story. Many years after his death he achieved an eminent place as one of the most influential writers in the world.

It was after his death that much of what he wrote influenced national leaders such as Mahatma Gandhi in India and Martin Luther King Jr. in America. Mahatma Gandhi took from Thoreau's "Civil Disobedience" the philosophy of passive resistance which led to India's freedom.

Thoreau's messages were those of harmony with nature,

simplicity of living, and civil liberty, and his quest for personal integrity was an ongoing journey which lasted his entire life.

Much of what concerned Thoreau in his time still is true today. Many people are still unhappy and are still trying to figure out how best to live their lives. This is why people still read a book called *Walden* and why they still remember a man named Henry David Thoreau.

Queen of the Underground Railroad

Harriet **Tubman**

"There are two things I have a right to. Either freedom or death. If I can't have one, then I will have the other."

—Harriet Tubman
(1820–1913)

Imagine this: You are a black female slave whose old master has died, and your new master is going to sell you and three of your brothers. You know there is a secret escape route to the North called the Underground Railroad, but you also know that the odds are against you if you try and escape. You have been told that escape is "impossible!"

Your name is Harriet Tubman, and you become an abolitionist, a humanitarian, and a Union spy. During the Civil War era you become known as the Queen of the Underground Railroad. Over and over again you risk your life to escort over three hundred slaves to freedom and you never lose any of them.

Harriet was born Araminta

(Minty) Ross around 1820 on a plantation in Maryland, one of eleven children, to Harriet Greene and Benjamin Ross, both slaves. Slave owners did not record their slaves' birthdays, and different accounts give her birthdate as 1820, 1821, and 1822.

By the early 1800s there were more than one and one-half million people living in slavery in the United States,[17] and Minty was one of those born into slavery. She knew only hard work and hunger, but she was different from many of the other slaves because she believed that she had a right to go free or die.

At age five she was hired out to neighbors to do housework by Mr. Edward Brodess, the owner of the plantation. She worked hard all day, and at night she slept by the fire, burying her feet in the ashes to keep them warm.

At age seven she was hired out to a woman to do chores during the day and to watch the woman's baby at night. When the baby cried at night and woke the mistress, Minty was whipped, and whenever she didn't do her chores well enough to please her mistress, she was whipped. She was whipped so often that she had scars on her neck for the rest of her life.

Minty was returned to Mr. Brodess who then sent her out to work in the fields. While she plowed the ground, hoed the weeds, chopped the wood, loaded the wagons, and took care of the mules, she listened to the field slaves talk about freedom and escape. And she sang about Moses in the Bible who had freed his people from slavery.

It was while working in the fields that Minty heard about the Underground Railroad, a network of people who led slaves to freedom in the North.

While helping another slave try to escape when she was thirteen, the man in charge of the slaves threw a heavy metal weight at the slave who was fleeing. It hit Minty instead, and she nearly died from a fractured skull.

When she recovered, she had a scar that marked her for life. People respected her courage, and they no longer called her by her nickname Minty. Instead, they began calling her by the name she had chosen—Harriet, her mother's name.

When she was about twenty-three, she married John Tubman, a free black man, but that didn't change her slave status. He refused to listen to her talk about freedom and told her that he would betray her if she ever tried to run away.

In 1849 her worst fears came true. The owner of the plantation died, and the plantation's bills were to be settled by selling some of its slaves. Two of her sisters had already been sold and were in chains.

Harriet persuaded three of her brothers to escape with her, but her brothers turned back in fear and forced her to return with them.

Two days later she found out she had been sold and knew that this time she would have to go alone. She had learned from her failed escape attempt that freedom is only for those bold enough to take it. If she could make it ninety miles to Philadelphia, she would be free.

Packing a little food, she set off into the woods after everyone was asleep. She waded through streams whenever possible so the bloodhounds couldn't follow her scent, and headed for the home of a Quaker woman whose home was a station on the Underground Railroad. The woman took her in and told her how to find the next station.

Harriet hid by day, sheltered by Quakers, and traveled at night guided by the North Star. One day she hid in an attic, another day she hid in a pile of potatoes under a cabin floor. One night she traveled in the bottom of a farmer's wagon, hidden under a pile of corn, and one night she crossed a river in a rowboat. Many nights she walked alone through the woods and the swamps.

For her last stop on the Underground Railroad, she met a conductor at a cemetery just outside Wilmington, Delaware. Mr. Trent was waiting for her with a shovel, a workman's hat, heavy shoes, and overalls to go over her long dress.

He told her to walk behind him like one of his workmen and not to say a word as they walked toward the bridge that led to Wilmington and where there were guards waiting and watching for runaway slaves.

Mr. Trent took her to a shop owned by Mr. Garrett who took her as far as he could in a buggy, then gave her directions for her last stop—Philadelphia, Pennsylvania.

At last she came to the small sign on a post by the road which had the same letters as the letters on the paper in her hand—*Philadelphia*.

Once on free soil, she looked at her hands to see if she was still the same person now that she was free. "When I found I had crossed that line, I looked at my hands to see if I was the same person. There was such a glory over everything."[18]

She sang and cried for joy as she walked down that free road toward Philadelphia, ninety miles from the plantation. "I'm free. I'm free at last!"

Harriet was free, but she didn't forget her people, and again and again, she risked her life to lead them on the same secret, dangerous journey. In 1850 she made the first of her nineteen trips into the South as a conductor on the Underground Railroad.

She worked as a scrubwoman in Philadelphia to earn money for the supplies she needed for her trips, and for seven years she traveled back and forth, bringing slaves safely to the North. One time, dressed as a man to fool the slave owners, she went back for her husband John. She was crushed to find that, although she had not forgotten him, he had forgotten her and had taken another wife.

She never learned to read or write, but she was a genius at planning every detail of a journey, from food and shelter to sleeping pills for crying babies, and she always managed to outsmart the slave owners. She developed an escape system, starting out with her group on a Saturday night. Since Sunday wasn't a work day, the runaways might not be missed until Monday.

People began calling her Moses after the biblical Moses who led his people out of slavery in Egypt. She traveled light and she traveled fast. She knew the places where it was safe to hide: drainage ditches, hedges, and abandoned sheds or tobacco barns. Sometimes she concealed her fugitives in potato holes, and once she and her group hid in a manure pile and breathed through straws.

As she grew famous, slave owners posted a forty-thousand-dollar reward for her capture, dead or alive. But she still kept making her trips. "I can't die but once," was her motto.

From 1850–1861, she made nineteen trips to the South. She led over three hundred slaves to freedom and never lost one. And she was never captured.

She became known by American leaders during the Civil War era as the Queen of the Underground Railroad. Then during the Civil War, she served for more than three years as spy, scout, nurse, and cook for the Union Army.

When the war ended, she returned home to her farm near Auburn, New York, where she cared for her parents.

The Emancipation Proclamation of 1863 freed slaves of the southern states, and her dream of freedom for her people came true with the passage of the Thirteenth Amendment in 1865 that outlawed slavery in all parts of the United States.

In her later years, she continued to devote her life to the needs of others, and her last cause was women's rights. "Tell the women to stand together,"[19] she said, a month before she died of pneumonia at approximately age ninety-three on March 10, 1913, in Auburn, New York.

Underground Railroad conductor, abolitionist, Union spy and nurse, and civil rights advocate—Harriet Tubman most definitely left her mark in American history.

The Angel of the Battlefield

Clara **Barton**

"I may sometimes be willing to teach for nothing, but if paid at all, I shall never do a man's work for less than a man's pay."

—Clara Barton
(1821–1912)

Imagine this: The Civil War has begun and you are very disturbed by all the wounded soldiers returning from the battlefields. You want to help, so you begin collecting donations of food, bandages, medicine, and clothing for the soldiers, and you want to deliver them yourself where they are most needed: on the battlefield. The War Department is shocked. Women can't be allowed on the battlefields!

Your name is Clarissa Harlowe Barton, and you are a teacher, nurse, and humanitarian. At great risk to yourself, you work tirelessly on the battlefield during the Civil War helping the wounded soldiers, and you insist on treating the Confederate soldiers as well as the Union soldiers. You eventually establish the American Red Cross and are named its first president.

Clarissa was born on Christmas Day 1821 in North Oxford, Massachusetts, the youngest of five children. Since her name seemed too fancy for everyday, she was called Clara. She was much younger than her brothers and sisters, and they doted on her—teaching her reading, writing, math, horseback riding, and carpentry.

Instead of being given toys or dolls, Clara was taught how to cook, sew, and run a house. Although she was a serious student, she preferred outdoor activities to the indoor pastimes "suitable" for young ladies at that time.

She was very bright but also extremely shy, and in an effort to cure her shyness, her parents sent her to boarding school. Lonely and homesick, she lost her appetite and stopped eating, so her family gave up and brought her home.

When she was eleven, her brother David fell from a roof while helping to build a barn. He was seriously injured, and for the next two years she nursed him back to health. Even back then she believed that if somebody were suffering, she must do something about it.

When she was sixteen, phrenologist Lorenzo Fowler advised her to become a teacher to cure her shyness, and for ten years she taught school in a small Massachusetts town.

At age eighteen, she took over a one-room schoolhouse where some of the older boys were bullies and had made their previous teacher's life miserable.

On the first day of school, Clara asked to join their games at recess. When they saw how fast she ran and how well she threw a ball, those boys or any of the other students gave her no problems after that.

She gained a reputation for being able to handle difficult

children, and she spent ten years visiting troubled schools and helping to resolve their problems.

While visiting Bordentown, New Jersey, she found that there were no free schools as there were in Massachusetts. If parents couldn't afford the tuition, their children couldn't go to school, so Clara offered to teach without pay if she were given a school. The very next day the school committee gave her a run-down, old building for her school. The first day of classes, only six students showed up, but after two years, the school had six hundred students and was housed in a brand new building.

The committee then decided that the school shouldn't be run by a woman and it hired a male principal. Clara was so angry that she left the school and the teaching profession. She moved to Washington, DC, where she became the first woman to work at the Patent Office and earn the same salary as the male clerks.

After Abraham Lincoln was elected president and the Civil War began, she became very disturbed by all the wounded soldiers returning from the battlefields, so she placed an ad in the newspaper asking for donations of food, bandages, medicine, and clothing. It wasn't long before she had more materials than she could store, and she wanted to deliver the supplies where they were most needed—on the battlefield.

The War Department was shocked. Women couldn't visit the battlefield! But she continued to ask until finally, in July 1862, she obtained permission to travel behind the lines, eventually reaching some of the grimmest battlefields of the war. She was given a pass for herself and three volunteers, and she was also given carts and teams of mules for carrying the supplies.

At the front, as bullets whizzed overhead and artillery boomed in the distance, she worked nonstop—cradling the heads of suffering Union soldiers, serving soup from laundry tubs, ladling out gallons of hot coffee, and overseeing the baking of hundreds of loaves of bread.

Since she knew many of the wounded men might not survive the long trip to a hospital, she began treating them right there on the battlefield, which was a radical new idea at the time.

She tended the sick in nursing stations set up in tents and wagons. She also insisted on treating Confederate solders from the enemy's army which shocked the War Department. The men called Clara the Angel of the Battlefield.

After the Civil War ended in 1865, she became a popular and widely respected lecturer. Also, she used her own money to set up an organization to trace missing soldiers and to identify the bodies of the dead.

In November 1867 she met Susan B. Anthony and Elizabeth Cady Stanton and found herself in complete sympathy with their struggle to win equal rights for women.

She wrote articles for Lucy Stone's *Woman's Journal* and occasionally appeared on the platform with Stanton, Anthony, Stone, and Julia Ward Howe at women's suffrage conventions. When she was unable to attend women's rights conventions, she often sent letters of support which were read to the audience.

Weakened by all her hard work, she left for Switzerland in 1869 to rest and regain her health.

In Geneva she learned about the Red Cross, an organization that helped the sick and wounded during wartime without respect to nationality.

Inspired by what she had learned about the Red Cross in Europe, she stressed a peacetime mission for the Red Cross: helping victims of floods, fires, earthquakes, droughts, hurricanes, and epidemics.

In 1881 at age sixty, Clara Barton helped to establish the American Red Cross and was named its first president.

In her sixties, she was still working as hard as ever. She spent five months living and working in a tent in Johnstown, Pennsylvania, after a terrible flood had ravaged the city.

And during the Spanish-American War, at age seventy-seven, she rode onto the battlefield in a wagon to feed and nurse the sick and set up orphanages for Cuban children whose parents had disappeared or been killed.

She continued to do relief work in the field well into her seventies, but she was not a strong administrator, and political feuding at the American Red Cross forced her to resign as president in 1904 when she was in her eighties.

When she died at the age of ninety-one, her body was taken from Glen Echo, Maryland, where she had been living, back to North Oxford, Massachusetts, for burial.

The carriage driver responsible for her casket told how Clara Barton had saved his father, a Confederate soldier, whom she had found bleeding to death on the battlefield. Now it was his turn to repay the kindness.[20]

Clara Barton is one of the most honored women in American history for being a true pioneer as well as an outstanding humanitarian. She began teaching school at a time when most teachers were men, and she risked her life when she was nearly forty years old to bring supplies and support to soldiers on the battlefields during the Civil War.

The Civil War was probably the primary defining event of her life as she discovered a real purpose for her life in nursing and in providing the relief of suffering.

Clara Barton has a well-earned place in American history as the Angel of the Civil War Battlefields and the founder of the American Red Cross.

Her intense devotion to helping others was her top priority all her life. Teacher, nurse, and humanitarian—the mission of her life can best be summed up in her own words, "You must never so much as think whether you like it or not, whether it is bearable or not; you must never think of anything except the need, and how to meet it."[21]

She Wanted to Do Something Important

Elizabeth Blackwell

"If Society will not admit of woman's free development, then society must be remodeled."

—Elizabeth Blackwell
(1821–1910)

Imagine this: You are a young woman who really wants to be a doctor, but there is a big problem. There are no women doctors because women are not admitted to medical schools. So what do you do?

Your name is Elizabeth Blackwell, and this is the situation you face in the 1800s. You don't want to give up your dream, so you apply to twenty-nine medical schools. You are turned down by twenty-eight of them, but the twenty-ninth accepts you, and you are on your way to fulfilling your dream. You become the first woman to receive a medical degree from a medical school in America, and you prepare the way for the women doctors who come after you.

Elizabeth was born in Bristol, England, in 1821, one of nine children. The Blackwells were a most unusual family because the principle of equality was a guiding rule in the Blackwell home. Elizabeth's parents, Samuel and Hannah, believed strongly in civil liberties and supported social reforms which included the abolition of slavery.

Unlike most English parents in the 1800s, Samuel and Hannah Blackwell believed that girls should be as well educated as boys and insisted that their sons and daughters be taught the same subjects. This meant that Elizabeth and her sisters studied the same subjects as their brothers, including history, astronomy, mathematics, and foreign languages.

When hard times came to England in 1831 and people lost their jobs, rioting broke out in Bristol. People were killed, buildings were set on fire, and the Blackwell family was deeply upset by the violence. Samuel saw little hope of saving his sugar refinery business without borrowing money, so he decided to make a fresh start in America where there were more opportunities.

Elizabeth was eleven when her family moved to America. They settled in New York City where her father built another sugar refinery, refusing to use slave labor.

As her father began to rebuild his business, the Blackwell family was faced with some of the same social problems they had back home, especially the problem of slavery. Elizabeth's family had always been opposed to slavery, and they opened their home to the abolitionists.

The Blackwell sisters were also drawn to another reform movement gaining strength in the United States during the 1800s—the Women's Movement for Equal Rights.

When Samuel suffered great losses during the financial depression of 1837, he moved his family from New York City to Cincinnati, Ohio, on the advice of a cousin.

Only three months after the move, Samuel became sick and died in August 1838, leaving the family destitute.

Elizabeth and her mother opened a boarding school in their home while Elizabeth's brothers and sisters also worked to help provide income for the family.

At age twenty-three Elizabeth was asked to take charge of a girls' school in Henderson, Kentucky. While in Kentucky, she was so upset by the treatment of the slaves and the proslavery attitudes of the South that she returned to Ohio within the year.

By age twenty-four she was longing for a purpose in life. She wanted to do something important. But she was a girl. What could she do?

Mary Donaldson, a family friend who was dying of cancer, finally convinced her that she could become a doctor. Somebody had to be the first woman doctor. Why not Elizabeth?

But when Elizabeth consulted several physicians, they were unanimous in their response: they all warned her that for a woman to become a doctor was impossible to accomplish.

Refusing to be discouraged by all the arguments against her becoming a doctor, she applied for admission to twenty-nine medical schools. She was turned down by twenty-eight of them.

Then finally, when she was twenty-six, little Geneva College in upstate New York, the twenty-ninth school, said **yes**!

She found out later that the Geneva medical students had been given the final say on her admission because everyone thought her application was a joke. No one had even taken it seriously.

When she arrived for classes in November 1847, everyone was most surprised! The students learned to like and respect her, but it was not so easy with the townspeople. They avoided her because they believed she was either crazy or "bad."

Curious strangers even visited her class lecture room just to stare at her.

In her own words, "I had not the slightest idea of the commotion created by my appearance as a medical student in the little town. Very slowly I perceived that a doctor's wife at the table avoided any communication with me, and that as I walked backwards and forwards to college, the ladies stopped to stare at me, as at a curious animal."[22]

As a female medical student, she felt a special commitment to her women patients. The more she saw how women patients were treated, the stronger her mission to help women became.

She graduated first in her class in 1849. She was now **Dr.** Blackwell, the first woman to receive a medical degree from a medical school in America. January 23, 1849, was a day that would forever change the world of medicine: Elizabeth Blackwell was about to become the very first woman doctor of modern times.

She then moved to Paris to continue her medical education, but while there, her dream of becoming a surgeon was shattered after she contracted a severe eye infection from an infected baby she was treating. Eventually her damaged left eye had to be replaced with a glass eye.

She then returned to England, but realizing that there were more opportunities for her in America, she returned to New York City in 1851.

At first, people did not want to go to a woman doctor. But she knew who really needed her—poor women and children. She opened a one-room clinic to serve women in 1853, and she did much more than treat sickness. She was a strong believer in preventive medicine and taught her patients the importance of good hygiene and nutrition. She believed that prevention was better than cure.

She worked very hard and by 1857 her clinic had grown into a hospital: The New York Infirmary for Women and Children. Elizabeth served as the director, her sister Emily was the clinic's surgeon, and Dr. Marie Zakrzewska was the resident physician. They ran a hospital for women and staffed entirely by women. At the time, male doctors and nurses made up 99 percent of the medical profession,[23] so this represented an extraordinary step in the history of medicine.

Women had been waiting for just such an opportunity, and within a month, all the beds were filled and dozens of patients showed up at the outpatient clinic. Other women could study to be nurses at her hospital, and in 1868 Elizabeth added a medical college for women which became known as the New York Infirmary for Women and Children and the Women's Medical College. Now other women could become doctors as well as nurses.

She continued to stress the importance of good personal hygiene because back then conditions in hospitals were very unsanitary. Doctors wore their street clothes, they didn't wash their hands between seeing patients, and rats even ran over patients' bodies at some hospitals.

In 1869 Elizabeth returned to London to help open the field of medicine for women there and helped found the London School of Medicine for Women. And in 1871 she started the National Health Society which helped people learn how to stay healthy.

When Elizabeth Blackwell earned her medical degree, this was a historic moment in modern medicine and women's liberation. She had challenged the medical world—and society's ideas about women—to become America's first female physician. The shy little girl had indeed done something important with her life.

By the time she died on May 31, 1910, at the age of eighty-nine, Elizabeth Blackwell had left a legacy that paved the way for countless generations of female physicians.

Physician, educator, reformer, and women's rights activist, Elizabeth Blackwell was a woman of vision who not only fulfilled her own impossible dream, but also made possible the dreams of the women who followed her.

The Forgotten Father of Technology

Nikola Tesla

"Science is but a perversion of itself unless it has as its ultimate goal the betterment of humanity."
—Nikola Tesla
(1856–1943)

Imagine this: You're twenty-eight years old, and you have just arrived in the United States with four cents in your pocket. Thanks to a strong letter of recommendation by a close friend of Thomas Edison, you're being interviewed by Edison himself at his Menlo Park research laboratory in New Jersey. But when you try to explain your invention of the induction motor which uses alternating current (AC) to Mr. Edison, he calls it "nonsense" and "dangerous." He tells you that he and all Americans are quite satisfied with direct current (DC) and plan to use no other system. Mr. Edison hires you, but he wants to hear no more nonsense about alternating current.

Your name is Nikola Tesla, and this is the situation you face when you arrive in the United States in 1884. Although you are hired by Edison, the differences in your beliefs persist, and you leave your job after a year. What follows is a titanic power struggle between Edison's direct-current systems and the Tesla-Westinghouse approach. You are destined to become one of the greatest scientists and inventors of the twentieth century, and during your lifetime you hold over seven hundred patents.

Tesla was born at midnight on July 10, 1856, in Smiljan, a small village in Croatia. The night of his birth was marked by a fierce thunderstorm and, and at the precise moment of his birth, the sky lit up with a huge bolt of lightning.

The midwife who had just delivered the new baby turned to Tesla's mother and said, "Your new son is a child of the storm." His mother responded by saying, "No, he is a child of the light."

He proved his mother right as he began to make original inventions as a young child. At age five, he built a small water-wheel quite unlike those he had seen in the countryside. It was smooth and without paddles, yet it spun evenly in the current.

And once he perched on the roof of the barn, clutching the family umbrella and hyperventilating until his body felt light and the dizziness in his head convinced him that he could fly. Plunging to earth, he lay unconscious and was carried off to bed by his mother.

Later Tesla attributed all of his inventive instincts to his mother who came from a family of inventors and who herself invented household appliances to help her with her home and farm responsibilities.

Even as a teenager, Tesla was very aware of the tremendous power of nature and hoped to some day harness this power for the good of humanity.

After completing his higher education at the University of Prague, he worked for the Edison Company in Paris before emigrating to the United States in 1884 with only four cents in his pocket.

He found employment with Thomas Edison at Edison's Menlo Park research laboratory in New Jersey, but differences in beliefs between the two men led to their separation a year later.

Tesla believed that alternating current was vastly superior to Edison's direct current because it could be altered or converted to suit a variety of situations.

In 1885 George Westinghouse, founder of the Westinghouse Electric Company, bought the patent rights to Tesla's system of alternating-current dynamos, transformers, and motors.

What ensued was a titanic power struggle between Edison's direct-current systems and the Tesla-Westinghouse alternating-current approach.

Tesla soon established his own laboratory where he gave dramatic demonstrations. Hoping to allay fears about alternating current, he lighted lamps without wires by allowing electricity to flow through his body.

By the time he became a United States citizen in 1891, he was at the peak of his creative powers. He had developed the induction motor, new types of generators and transformers, a system of alternating-current power transmission, fluorescent lights, and a new type of steam turbine.

Although his inventions received many awards, he always considered his United States citizenship more important than any of the scientific awards he received.

Around this time, Tesla developed a close and lasting friendship with the author Samuel Clemens (Mark Twain), and they spent a lot of time together in Tesla's lab.

Tesla later told Clemens how his books had saved his life when he was a boy of twelve struck down with a potentially fatal case of malaria. Clemens was so moved by Tesla's story that tears came to his eyes.[24]

Tesla drove himself so tirelessly that his friends worried about his health, but nothing and no one could slow him down. He continued to invite his friends to his laboratory to witness his experiments and Samuel Clemens was one of his most frequent guests.

The Tesla coil, invented in 1891, was one of his most famous inventions. Tesla coils are unique in the fact that they create extremely powerful electrical fields, and they're widely used today in radio and television sets and other electronic equipment.

The advantages of alternating current over Edison's system of direct current became apparent when Westinghouse successfully used Tesla's system to light the World Columbian Exposition at Chicago in 1893.

His success there led to a contract to install the first power machinery at Niagara Falls. By building generators that used Tesla's alternating-current system to harness the power of Niagara Falls, Westinghouse demonstrated that not only could Tesla's discoveries be put to practical use but also that alternating current was one of the greatest discoveries of all time.

Tesla had a photographic memory as well as a vivid imagination, and he had a most unusual and intuitive way of developing his scientific hypotheses. Throughout his life, he maintained the uncanny ability to design, build, and test an invention in his head before actually putting it on paper or building it in the lab.

He once said that it didn't matter whether he devised his inventions in his head or in the laboratory because they worked just as well either way. And they did!

Tesla was responsible for a great many other inventions and devices that we take for granted today. He claimed the ability to locate objects in the air or on the ground by using radio waves which today we call *radar*. These waves can also be used to examine the inside of the human body by what we now call an MRI (Magnetic Resonance Imaging).

With his theory of alternating current, he had focused on a fundamental force of nature and discovered the key to the safe and economical industrial application of electricity.

Unfortunately, he did not always receive recognition for his efforts. Even today, many still credit Guglielmo Marconi with the invention of the radio despite the 1943 Supreme Court decision that overruled the Marconi patent and awarded it to Tesla.[25]

Although it was Tesla who harnessed the alternating electrical current we use today and fundamentally changed the world, he is frequently included only as a footnote to the stories of the more renowned inventors and industrialists of his day such as Thomas Edison and George Westinghouse.

He was a visionary genius whose discoveries ushered in the modern industrial age, but he was in large part also the Forgotten Father of Technology.

Nikola Tesla was one of the twentieth century's greatest scientists and inventors. He not only discovered the rotating magnetic field, the basis of most alternating-current machinery, but he also introduced us to the fundamentals of robotics, remote control, radar, computer science, and missile science and expanded our knowledge of ballistics, nuclear physics, and theoretical physics.

Even though at the time of his death in 1943, he held over seven hundred patients, he died nearly penniless because of serious financial setbacks.

When he died in New York City on January 7, 1943, at age

eighty-six, two thousand admirers attended his funeral services to mourn the loss of a great genius.

Inventor, mechanical engineer, and electrical engineer, Tesla was a true visionary far ahead of his contemporaries in the field of scientific development.

Booker T. Washington

"I will permit no man to narrow and degrade my soul by making me hate him."

—Booker T. Washington (1856–1915)

Imagine this: You are born a black slave in Virginia and, more than anything, you want to go to school. But since it's against the law to educate slaves, you aren't even taught to read or write. In spite of the odds against you, however, you never give up your dream for an education.

Your name is Booker T. Washington, and you end up not only getting a college education yourself, but also helping other black citizens receive an education. Under your leadership, the Tuskegee Institute becomes one of the most famous schools in America. You are later remembered for helping black Americans rise up from the economic slavery that held them down long after they were legally free citizens.

Washington was born a slave on the Burroughs tobacco farm in Virginia, and, because slave records were seldom kept back then, his birth date can only be estimated as 1856. His mother was a cook and his father was a white man from a near-by farm whom Washington never knew.

The squalid conditions in which he lived were common-place for slaves: a one-room, dirt-floored cabin 14 × 16 feet with no windows and only a fireplace for cooking and heating. He and his family slept on rags heaped on the floor.

More than anything he wanted to go to school, but since it was against the law to educate slaves, he wasn't even taught to read or write.

He said later that his first realization that he was a slave came early one morning as a young boy when he awoke to find his mother praying over her children that Lincoln's armies would win and that one day she and her family would be free.[26]

When the Civil War ended in 1865, his mother's prayer was answered, and his family moved to West Virginia where his stepfather had found work in the salt mines.

For Washington, freedom meant one thing: now he could go to school. But his stepfather had a different idea. The fami-ly needed money, so Washington had to work in the salt mines along with his brother and stepfather from dawn to nine o'clock at night with very few breaks during the day.

While working in the salt mines, each salt packer was given a barrel marked with a number and his father's number was 18. Booker learned to recognize that number and to write it.

From that time on he had an intense longing to read and persuaded his mother to get hold of a book for him. Somewhere his mother found an old Webster's spelling book, and it became his most treasured possession. The book contained the alphabet, and he studied that book until he had mastered the entire alphabet.

In his autobiography he later wrote, "In all my efforts to learn to read my mother shared fully my ambition, and sympathized with me and aided me in every way that she could."[27]

Though his mother was totally ignorant as far as book knowledge was concerned, she had high ambitions for her children, and Washington later said that the lessons in virtue and thrift she taught him remained with him all his life. No one was stricter than his mother in teaching and observing the highest rules of integrity.

To support the teacher at the black school that had opened in their community, parents of the students took turns feeding and boarding him in their homes.

Even though Washington wasn't a student because he had to work, his mother still agreed to invite the teacher to join them for meals one day each month. And soon Washington was receiving private lessons at night.

His stepfather finally agreed to let Washington go to school a few months of the year, but only if he continued to work from four o'clock until nine o'clock in the morning and then return to work in the mines for a few more hours after school. Washington later said that his first day at school was the happiest day of his life.

All the other boys wore caps to school, but his mother couldn't afford to buy him one, so she sewed two pieces of cloth together and that was his cap. The other boys teased him about his crude homemade cap, but Booker wore it proudly.

Regarding that incident, he later wrote that that was an important lesson his mother had taught him. She had the strength of character to do what she could for him, but she refused to worry about trying to impress his schoolmates and others with the fact that she was able to buy him a "store hat" when she was not.

Unable to keep up the grueling schedule, he soon had to drop out of school and work all day at the salt mines.

When he was about twelve, he went to work in a coal mine where one day he heard two men talking about a new school for African Americans, a school set up by whites to educate African Americans after the Civil War.

It was called the Hampton Institute, and black students could go there even if they didn't have any money. They could pay their way by working at the school. Washington didn't know where Hampton was or how to get there. He only knew that somehow he would go to this school.

No one sympathized with his ambition to go to Hampton more than his mother, but even she feared that he might be starting out on a wild-goose chase. He did get her half-hearted consent, however, so he started out.

It took him weeks to make his way the five hundred miles to Hampton all on his own, walking most of the way. Once there, the female principal told him to sweep a room for her. He knew it was a test, so he swept and dusted the room three times until not a speck of dirt remained. He was accepted into the school, and he had attained his "impossible" dream.

While at the Hampton Institute, he worked as a janitor to pay his way, and he learned important lessons about education that would stay with him the rest of his life. He learned that cleanliness was an important part of one's self-worth, that education did not mean that one was above manual labor, and that one should lead by example.

One teacher, Miss Nathalie Lord, gave him lessons in public speaking which helped him a great deal later on in attaining financial and moral support for his work.

After graduating from Hampton, he returned to his hometown and taught day school, night classes, and two Sunday schools. In 1881 he was selected to be the principal of a new school for African Americans in Alabama called Tuskegee. When its doors opened on July 4, 1881, the school was little more than a broken down shanty and an old henhouse with one teacher and thirty students.

Under Washington's leadership, the Tuskegee Institute grew into one of the most famous schools in America. He always stressed the importance of cleanliness and spirituality and that there was no shame in being a laborer. He believed that "no race can prosper till it learns that there is as much dignity in tilling a field as in writing a poem."[28]

The emphasis at Tuskegee was on the trades and daily living skills. He believed in educating the "head, hand, and the heart," and he hoped that his graduates would go throughout the country and be an example to all who came in contact with them.

He told his students to build their own houses so they would not be homeless and to grow food and raise animals so they would never be hungry.

Washington's enormous capacity for hard work and his success in winning financial and moral support in the cause of Negro education earned him a national reputation as the outstanding black leader of his day.

In 1896, Washington was awarded an honorary master's degree from Harvard, the nation's oldest university. He had come a long way since his childhood as an impoverished slave who dreamed of one day learning to read.

When Washington died in 1915 at age fifty-nine, he was one of the most well known (black or white) men in the world, and more than eight thousand people attended his funeral held in the Tuskegee Institute Chapel.

They Stood Alone!

This extraordinary black educator who was born a slave overcame near-impossible odds to become one of the most powerful black leaders of his time.

Washington believed that the way to gain equality was through education, and his name still brings to mind leadership, academic excellence, and the ongoing pursuit of equality for everyone.

The Woman Who Changed the Course of Science

Marie Curie

"Nothing in life is to be feared. It is only to be understood."

—Marie Curie
(1867–1934)

Imagine this: You are a young Polish woman whose dream is to become a scientist, but in Poland women aren't even allowed to go to universities. So what do you do?

Your name is Marie Curie, and you are accepted to the Sorbonne, the prestigious University of Paris, when you are twenty-four and become the first woman to receive a master's degree in physics from the Sorbonne. You also become the first woman to teach at the Sorbonne and the first woman to hold the rank of full professor in the scientific world. You are also the first person to receive the Nobel Prize twice and for two different sciences—first physics, then chemistry. You are later described all over the world as the Polish French scientist whose work put humanity on a new scientific course.

Marie was born Maria Sklodowska in Warsaw, Poland, on November 7, 1867, the youngest of five children. Her father was a professor of mathematics and physics, and her mother had been the director of a girls' boarding school.

The family focus was on education and serving others, and they believed that learning was the most exalted goal in anyone's life. They believed that learning would keep Poland's intellect alive and restore her independence as the Polish people were struggling under the crushing yoke of the Russian tsars who ruled over them.

Marie was just a young girl when she lost both her mother to tuberculosis and her sister Zosia to typhus. To cope with these painful losses, the children pretended they were genius doctors who discover a miracle cure.

Marie was the star pupil in her class at Warsaw's Pension Sikorska, a private school for girls. And it was Marie who saved her classmates, her teacher, and the director of the school from possible Siberian exile when Mr. Hornberg, the Russian school inspector, made one of his surprise visits.[29]

The school inspectors made surprise visits to the school, hoping to catch the students studying Polish history and speaking Polish which were forbidden by the tsar.

When the inspector demanded answers to his questions about Russian history, Marie responded correctly in perfect Russian. She could also have responded In German, English, or French as well.

Her dream was to study physics at the University of Paris (the Sorbonne), the most distinguished school of science in the world, so she and her older sister Bronia made a pact. Marie would work and help support Bronia through medical school and then after graduation, Bronia would help support Marie.

Finally, in September 1891, eight years after graduating at the top of her high school class, she was ready to continue her own education. With the blessings of her father, she packed her clothes and moved to Paris where she lived in a tiny, bare attic room—freezing in the winter and broiling in the summer.

Two months later, having passed the exams, she was accepted as a student of physics at the Sorbonne. A brilliant student, she graduated first in her class with a degree in physics in 1893, the first woman to receive a master's degree in physics from the Sorbonne.

She was hired in 1894 to do a study of the magnetic properties of steel. It was then that she met Pierre Curie, a noted physicist and the manager of the laboratory where she would conduct her research.

Pierre and Marie spent every spare minute together discussing science and, a year later, they were married.

In 1896 another scientist, named Antoine Henri Becquerel, told the Curies about the glowing rays he had seen in a brown lump of uranium ore called *pitchblende*, and Pierre suggested that Marie use that for the subject of her doctoral degree.

Marie began testing chemical elements to identify the substance causing the glow. A year later she concluded that the mysterious substance was an unknown "radiant" element.

She and Pierre announced the discovery of this new element in July 1898, and she named it *polonium* for her native country Poland.

But there was something more powerful still trapped in the pitchblende. Later that year, on December 26, the Curies announced the existence of a second element, more highly radioactive than any other known. They named it *radium*.

To prove the existence of these new elements, they needed to isolate enough of each element from the pitchblende in order to measure the precise atomic weight (the weight of one atom of an element) of each element.

Over the next four years, she and Pierre labored in an old, leaky shed and finally, in 1902, she produced one-tenth of a gram of pure radium from a ton of pitchblende.

The amount was like a teardrop in the ocean, yet its glow was a million times stronger than that of uranium rays. What awesome power lay in the atomic structure of that element!

At the time scientists believed that atoms of elements were unchangeable whereas the Curies were proving that the atoms of radioactive elements were constantly changing and even transforming from one element into a completely different one. As atoms of radioactive elements changed from one element into another (the decay process), they released energy which Marie called "radioactivity."

On June 25, 1903, having submitted her paper "Researches on Radioactive Substances," she was formally awarded her doctor of physical science degree—the first woman in France to be awarded the doctorate of science degree.

In November 1903, the Nobel Prize in Physics was awarded to Henri Becquerel and to the Curies for their work on radioactivity—the first Nobel Prize awarded to a woman.

The following year, Pierre was appointed full professor at the Sorbonne and given a laboratory with three assistants. One was Marie, the most celebrated woman of science in the world.

When Pierre was killed in April 1906 in an unfortunate accident, Marie replaced him at the Sorbonne. She was given only the rank of assistant professor, but she was still the first woman ever to teach at the Sorbonne.

Two years later, in 1908, she was promoted to full professor, becoming the first woman to hold such high rank in the scientific world.

In 1911 she was proposed for membership in the French Academy of Science, but her name was rejected when one member insisted that women could not be included in the membership.

Later that year she was awarded the Nobel Prize in Chemistry for the discovery and isolation of polonium and radium which she dedicated to her husband's memory. This was the first time anyone had received the Nobel Prize twice and for two different sciences—first physics, then chemistry.

Marie's only wish was to see Pierre's and her work used to improve the human condition, especially to cure cancer. It was her hope that by exposing diseased tissue to controlled radium rays, illnesses such as cancer could be conquered.

In 1914 she was appointed the director of the Radium Institute in Paris; students and technicians came to the institute from around the world. Among them were young Poles whose expenses were secretly paid by Marie.

She also took to the battlefields of France during World War I from 1914 to 1918 with her daughter Irene in a truck loaded with X-ray and radium therapy equipment. Over one million wounded soldiers were X-rayed for bullets and shrapnel and, knowing exactly where to operate, doctors were able to save countless lives.

In 1921 Marie made her first trip to the United States where President Warren Harding presented her with a gram of radium purchased with a collection taken up by American women.

In 1922 she was elected to the French Academy of Medicine for her contributions to radiological medicine, the only woman so recognized.

In 1925 she returned to Warsaw, now the capital of Poland, to lay the cornerstone of the Radium Institute of Warsaw.

She died nine years later on July 4, 1934, at age sixty-six of leukemia, brought on by her years of exposure to high levels of radiation. After her death the Radium Institute of Warsaw was renamed the Curie Institute.

Marie Curie explored the nature of uranium rays, coined the term *radioactivity*, discovered the elements polonium and radium, and isolated pure radium for the first time.

The Curies unlocked the secrets of the atom and revolutionized modern science which ushered in the nuclear age.

Mohandas **Gandhi**

"We must be the change we wish to see in the world."

— Mahatma Gandhi
(1869–1948)

Imagine this: It's 1893 and you are a twenty-four-year-old Indian lawyer practicing in South Africa. While taking a train, you are asked to leave your first-class compartment and go to the third-class compartment because of the color of your skin. You refuse because you have paid for a first-class ticket. You're forcefully removed from the train, your luggage is confiscated, and you're left in the bitterly cold waiting room of the railway station with only a small suitcase. What do you do? Do you fight for your rights or do you return to India and forget the injustices in South Africa?

Your name is Mohandas Gandhi, and you decide it would be cowardly to return to India, so you remain in South Africa for twenty-two years where you fight an ongoing battle for racial tolerance and become one of the most influential and well-respected political and social leaders the world has ever known.

Gandhi was born on October 2, 1869, in Porbandar, India, the youngest of four children and was influenced by his father's politics and his mother's religion.

He was a small, shy boy, afraid of many things, including the dark, and had to sleep with the lights on.

In 1887 his family reluctantly allowed him to leave India to study law in London, and to satisfy his mother he made a solemn vow not to touch wine, women, or meat. Despite his attempts to fit in, he still felt like an outcast in the city.

He felt very much alone, a foreigner in a strange country. To try to feel more comfortable and secure, he transformed himself into an English gentleman—living in fancy rooms and wearing fancy clothes. He learned to speak perfect English, took violin lessons, and even learned how to dance.[30]

But he still felt a deep conflict between his inner self and his outer self. Remembering the values of his home, he tried to live a simpler life. He gave up his fancy rooms, cooked his own meals, walked everywhere he went, and joined the Vegetarian Society of London. His changes made him much happier, although he still remained awkward and shy.

He finally passed his law exams and, after three years in London, he returned home to India in 1891 to set up a law practice in Bombay. His shyness and problems with the Indian courts, however, led him to accept a low-paying position as a legal adviser in South Africa in 1893 where he experienced racism firsthand.

Traveling by train to Pretoria shortly after his arrival in South Africa, he was told to leave the first class car, for which he had a ticket, because he wasn't white. When he refused to go to another compartment, he was thrown off the train.

Outraged by the experience, he resolved to fight back legally. Overcoming his shyness, he sued the railroad and won a grudging victory. The law was then changed so that all Indians could sit in the seat to which their tickets entitled them, provided they wore English-style clothing.

Word of this victory spread quickly, and Gandhi soon became a champion of Indian rights in South Africa and, indirectly, a spokesperson for all the powerless.

He remained in South Africa for the next twenty-two years, working to end the country's discriminatory legislation against people of color.

The legal work was hard but rather than quit and leave an unfriendly country, he decided to look on every difficulty as an opportunity for service to others. This was to be the secret of his success for the rest of his life.

He was determined to root out the disease of prejudice, but never to yield to violence. He vowed to bring the peace of heaven to earth.

At the turn of the twentieth century, South Africa was ruled by the Dutch, and on August 22, 1906, the Dutch government passed the Black Act, which deprived black and Indian people of their civil rights. In response, Gandhi formed his first non-violent mass resistance movement, and over five hundred people participated in this movement of civil disobedience.

Gandhi and his followers worked for the rights of black and Indian people and also for the rights of women. He did legal work for free, nursed sick people abandoned during a plague, and comforted the dying. He believed that all people were his brothers and sisters and that their suffering was his suffering.

By believing in the power of love and treating everyone as

his family, he discovered that he was no longer shy and no longer afraid of anything.

When he returned to India in 1915, he began the struggle for India's independence. He wanted to rid India of its caste system that placed priests at the highest social level, which meant that they were treated better than anyone else in the country. The next level was reserved for princes and soldiers, laborers at a third level, and the poor—the "untouchables"—at the fourth and lowest level.

He also worked to rid India of British oppression. For three hundred years, several thousand British people had ruled over 300 million Indian people. Gandhi spoke to millions of people, asking them to practice the selfless love of *satyagraha*, a word which means truth and persistence.

Indians ceased to cooperate with the British and many were jailed. Many even spun their own cloth so they wouldn't have to purchase British-made cloth. The white, homespun cloth called *kadhi* was worn by millions of people and became the symbol of Indian independence.

From 1920 on, Gandhi organized campaigns of civil disobedience, always based on nonviolent methods.

In 1922 the British imprisoned Gandhi for two years for defying British rule and writing anti-British pamphlets. But his time in prison didn't deter him from his dream to make every man and woman in India free.

The British were so oppressive in India that they even controlled the products Indians bought and used every day. In hot, tropical countries like India, salt is an essential part of everyone's diet. However, British law in India forbade Indians from making their own salt, forcing them to buy salt from the British. Because of these unfair laws, in 1930 Gandhi led the Salt March. Accompanied by seventy-eight people, he began his walk from Sabarmati to Dandi, a town on the ocean over two hundred miles away.

By the time he reached Dandi and picked up a pinch of sea salt in symbolic defiance of British rule, he had been joined by thousands of people. The British government was forced to acknowledge that it was losing its stronghold on India.

People began to eulogize Gandhi and call him Mahatma, a term of respect meaning the Great Soul.

In 1932 he was imprisoned again and embarked on his "epic fast unto death" to protest British rule and official discrimination against the untouchables. It was a powerful and nonviolent way of threatening the British government. They didn't want to be responsible for Gandhi's death, so after six days, the government agreed to a pact to protect the civil rights of the untouchables. This kind of social change brought about by peaceful means was a great victory for Gandhi.

On August 12, 1947, India finally won its independence from British rule, but the country was divided into two separate countries—Hindu India to the south and Muslim Pakistan to the north.

Gandhi did not celebrate India's independence because of his country's division. He yearned for his people to overcome hatred with love. Just as his *satyagraha* movement had enabled India to overcome British rule, Gandhi hoped this movement would unify the factions that now divided India. But such unification was not to be.

Because he taught unity and the brotherhood of people of all religions, he was hated by those Hindus and Muslims who believed their own religion was the only true religion.

Gandhi remained a firm champion of tolerance to the very end of his life. On the evening of January 30, 1948, as he walked to a prayer meeting where thousands of people awaited him, a young Hindu dissident named Nathuram Godse fired a gun at his heart and Gandhi fell. His last words were of forgiveness to his killer.

Although he died feeling he had failed in his mission to create a free and United India, he had inspired other leaders to pick up his torch. Both Martin Luther King Jr.'s nonviolent civil rights movement in the United States and Nelson Mandela's anti-apartheid movement in South Africa used Gandhi's techniques of civil disobedience and nonviolent, passive resistance to protest racial segregation and injustice.

Gandhi's philosophies of nonviolence and peaceful protest had inspired people around the world and changed the lives of millions.

The Flying Duo

Orville **Wright**

"If birds can glide for long periods of time, then... why can't I?"

—Orville Wright (1871–1948) with his brother Wilbur Wright (1867–1912)

Imagine this: It's 1896 and you're seriously ill with typhoid fever. Your brother is at your bedside reading an article about the death of a famous German glider pilot and, because of this article, your lives will never be the same again.

Your name is Orville Wright, and you and your brother Wilbur become obsessed with the idea of inventing a machine that can fly. You believe that if you can make something go at a certain speed with enough thrust and create an aerodynamic force, you can transcend the law of gravity.

Orville Wright was born in Dayton, Ohio, on August 19, 1871, one of five children, and his older brother Wilbur was born in Millville, Indiana, on April 16, 1867.

Their father, Milton, was a minister and their mother, Susan, could build or fix almost anything, skills both brothers inherited. They looked to their mother for mechanical expertise and to their father for intellectual challenge.

Their father held some strong and unusual ideas about education that helped shape his children's lives. He encouraged attention to detail by demanding long, very specific letters from his children during his frequent absences from home. And his method of fostering independence was to advise the boys to take a day off from school now and then.

Even from early childhood, both Orville and Wilbur were interested in any kind of mechanical device. When Orville was in kindergarten, the family was stunned to learn that, though he left home and returned when he was expected to, he did not go to kindergarten. Instead, he stopped each morning at the home of a neighbor boy where they could play with an old sewing machine.[31]

When Orville was in his teens, he worked for a printer for two summers and then opened his own print shop. In 1889 Orville's dream of publishing a newspaper came true with the publication of the *West Side News*, a weekly paper. Wilbur edited the paper while Orville printed and sold it.

Then, deciding they wanted a new challenge, they opened a bicycle repair shop in 1892. Three years later they created the Wright Cycle Company to manufacture bicycles.

In August 1896 Orville became seriously ill with typhoid fever. While Wilbur was reading at Orville's bedside, he came across an article about the German inventor and engineer Otto Lilienthal and his flying machine. After that, life would never be the same for the Wright brothers.

Both brothers caught the flying bug, and in May 1899 Wilbur wrote to the Smithsonian Institution in Washington,

DC, requesting any information they might have on the subject of flying.

Convinced that there must be a way for humans to fly, they spent many hours watching birds in flight. They noticed that some birds were able to soar for long periods of time without flapping their wings and wondered how this was possible.

They studied all the inventors who had tried to build flying machines and observed that curved wings, like those of the birds, apparently developed more lift than flat ones. So they built a double-winged glider which they intended to fly as a kite.

Now they had an opportunity to learn about lift and control with no danger to themselves. They reasoned that if they could make a set of wings that would develop lift and could be controlled, they could simply build bigger and better wings until they had a set large enough to lift a man.

It soon became clear to the brothers, however, that if they followed their plan to build and fly bigger gliders, the fields around Dayton wouldn't be large enough.

The United States Weather Bureau suggested the Outer Banks of North Carolina. Those long, narrow islands seemed perfect for the experiments. The wind off the ocean blew steadily almost all the time, and as far as you could see, there was nothing but gently sloping dunes and occasional large hills of soft sand.

They spent the winter of 1899 and the spring and summer of 1900 building a large glider. Late that summer they took the glider apart, packed all the pieces and parts into a large shipping trunk, and set off for the village of Kitty Hawk, North Carolina, where in 1900 they began testing their glider.

Flying the glider as a kite, they added weight a little at a time and soon found that the glider could lift no more than seventy-five pounds, which was barely half the lift they needed.

After they changed the curvature several times, the wings developed enough lift to carry the brothers, one at a time, on short glides down the slope of a large sand dune.

The more they studied the problem, the more sure they were that the curvature of the wings was at the heart of the problem, so they returned to Dayton to find a solution.

They made another adjustment in the curvature of the wings and then returned to Kitty Hawk in 1901 with their new, revised glider to try again. The change in wing shape made all the difference, and the glider was actually able to gain enough speed to maintain itself in flight.

Now the brothers turned their attention to the problem of control. Once again in Dayton, they built a wind tunnel to test their various theories about why their glider wouldn't turn. Returning to Kitty Hawk in the late summer of 1902, they now had a glider that they hoped would respond to turns. And on October 2, 1902, the machine responded well.

Now they just had to find a motor that was light enough and powerful enough to get the glider off the ground. Since no motor meeting their specifications was available, they built one themselves in their machine shop back in Dayton.

Neither brother had any formal education beyond high school, yet in just three and one-half years—from 1899 when they wrote to the Smithsonian until the autumn of 1902 when they solved the problems of lift and control—they had become the most knowledgeable people in the world about flying.

They had not only discovered major errors in the theories of flight, but they had also researched, tested, and proved that their own ideas were correct.

During the winter of 1902–1903 they worked on the machine that was to become the world's first airplane. They decided to use two propellers turning in opposite directions, and they scaled up their glider drawings to accommodate the additional weight of the motor.

On September 23, 1903, the brothers left Dayton for their third trip to Kitty Hawk with what Wilbur called their "whopper flying machine." Twenty-one feet long, wings stretching more than forty feet from tip to tip, the entire airplane weighed 605 pounds.

On December 14, 1903, the brothers tossed a coin to decide who would have the honor of making the first try. Wilbur won the toss and settled himself into the hip cradle on the lower wing. The "flight" lasted just three and one-half seconds as the airplane rolled forward forty feet, climbed fifteen feet into the air, and then sank back onto the sand, splintering several pieces of its wooden structure in the process.

They repaired the plane and on Friday, December 17, 1903, it was Orville's turn to try. Though the *Flyer* went only 120 feet and was in the air only twelve seconds, it had actually flown!

Orville had flown the airplane from a standstill under its own power, he had maintained control long enough to prove that it could be done, and he had landed the *Flyer* safely.

At 11:20 that morning, Wilbur completed a flight of 175 feet in twelve seconds. Twenty minutes later, Orville stayed in the air for fifteen seconds and flew 200 feet.

The world's First Flight had taken place on Friday, December 17, 1903, and was indeed a great moment in aviation. The rest, as they say, is history.

The present state of flight would not have been possible without the brothers' determination, drive, and perseverance.

Years after the success of the *Flyer*, Orville was devastated by the death of Wilbur in 1912 at age forty-five from typhoid fever. Despite Orville's sadness, continued to work on his inventions and experiments and on April 8, 1930, he was awarded the first Daniel Guggenheim Medal, an award given for great achievements in aeronautics. He died on January 30, 1948, at age seventy-six from a heart attack.

No matter how fast, no matter how big, and no matter how powerful the airplanes we use today, they are all direct descendants of that fragile, white-winged glider-with-a-motor that was the first successful powered airplane. The method of flight control that the Wright brothers developed remains the basis of all fixed-wing air transportation today.

The Father of Modern Physics

Albert Einstein

"The most incomprehensible thing about the world is that it is at all comprehensible."

—Albert Einstein
(1879–1955)

Imagine this: Although Newton's law of universal gravity still provides extremely accurate explanations of physical observations, you have a major issue with his theory because it's not consistent with your own special theory of relativity which predicts that space and time are **relative**, forming a four-dimensional continuum you call spacetime.

Your name is Albert Einstein, and you revolutionize our concepts of space, time, matter, energy, and light. Except for perhaps Nicolaus Copernicus and Isaac Newton, no one else so changes the way we see our physical world. You are considered one of the greatest scientists of all time and receive the Nobel Prize in Physics.

Einstein was born March

14, 1879, in Ulm, Germany, and he was so slow to learn to speak that his parents wondered if he might be "mildly retarded." Behind his back, the family maid referred to him as "the dopey one."[32]

He was no model child. At age five he threw a chair at a tutor who then quit on the spot. He also threw things at his little sister Maja and was not very sociable, preferring to go his own way and do his own thing.

Although his family was Jewish, he attended a Catholic elementary school where, as the only Jewish student, he was sometimes bullied.

There's a persistent myth that he did poorly in school and even failed math, but published copies of his report cards show that he got good grades in everything, including math.

He was always a rebellious and independent thinker and resented having to memorize and learn things by rote. He preferred to learn things on his own in his own way, and he often told people that his thoughts came to him in pictures rather than in words.

By the time he was fifteen, he was focused on science—especially physics with its new ideas about magnetism and electricity and light. He said later that that was the year he became convinced that nature could be understood as a relatively simple mathematical structure.

He dropped out of school at fifteen, three years before his graduation, partly because he hated school but also because of his family's financial problems.

After he left school in 1894, he joined his family in Italy and renounced his German citizenship. He then belonged to no country until he became a Swiss citizen in 1901.

He failed the entrance exam the first time he applied for admission to the Swiss Federal Institute of Technology in

Zurich, Switzerland, because although he did brilliantly in math and physics, he failed dismally in literature, zoology, botany, and French.

When he was finally accepted by the Swiss Federal Institute of Technology in 1896, his academic record was never brilliant because he spent most of his time and energy on his own studies rather than on the studies assigned by the institute. He didn't care for such organized education, and he hated having to attend classes regularly and take exams.

This independent spirit later cost him a much needed job at the institute after graduation, and he was the only one in his graduating class who was not offered an appointment as an assistant professor at the institute.

Aside from his grades being just average, he had antagonized some of his professors with his rebellious and independent attitude, and they refused to write any letters of recommendation for him.

After his graduation in 1900, he had difficulty finding a job, so he took temporary teaching jobs. Then in 1902, with the help of a friend, he got a job with the Swiss Patent Office where he found time to pursue his own interests in physics and higher mathematics.

In 1905 he laid the groundwork for the atomic age by developing the formula $E = mc^2$ (energy = mass times the speed of light squared) which became probably the most famous formula in science.

He published four papers in 1905 which revolutionized scientists' understanding of the universe. Space and time were redefined. He believed that energy and matter were basically the same thing and that you could convert one into the other. Much like Isaac Newton's memorable year of 1666, the year 1905 was a "miracle year" for Einstein.

What Einstein called his special theory of relativity was considered by other scientists to be one of the most significant pieces of scientific work ever done. He had shown for the first time that there was a relationship between matter and energy and that one could be converted into the other.

He became world famous for his special theory of relativity in 1905 and for his general theory of relativity in 1916 which became the basis of modern nuclear development.

On May 29, 1919, a solar eclipse proved that his general theory of relativity worked. During a total solar eclipse, Sir Arthur Eddington, a British physicist, performed the first experimental test of Einstein's general theory of relativity. His findings made Einstein a celebrity overnight and prepared the way for the eventual triumph of general relativity over classical Newtonian physics.

Although Newton's law of universal gravity still provided extremely accurate explanations of physical observations, Einstein had a major issue with Newton's theory because it wasn't consistent with his own special theory of relativity which predicted that space and time were **relative**, forming a four-dimensional continuum he called spacetime.

Einstein's research papers had forever changed mankind's view of the universe, and on December 10, 1922, he was awarded the 1921 Nobel Prize for Physics.

As important as his research was to him, he was also just as passionate about striving for international peace. As a Jew, Einstein spoke out against Nazi crimes against Jews and consequently became very unpopular with the Nazis in Germany. After the Nazis came to power in 1933 and seized his property, he never returned to Germany.

Instead, he settled in Princeton, New Jersey, where he was welcomed at the Institute for Advanced Study at Princeton University and where he attempted to unify the laws of physics.

In 1939 with the advent of World War II, he wrote his famous letter to President Franklin D. Roosevelt. In it he warned of the possibility of Germany building an atomic bomb and urged more nuclear research which inspired President Roosevelt to accelerate the US nuclear program to compete and win against the Axis Powers.

His work led indirectly to the development of the atomic bomb which saddened him, as he had not intended his work to be used for destructive purposes.

In 1940 he became an American citizen while still retaining his Swiss citizenship. He spent his latter years campaigning for the control of nuclear weapons and for the peaceful use of atomic energy. Then in 1945 he was appointed chairman of the Emergency Committee of Atomic Scientists dedicated to furthering world peace.

In 1952 he was offered the Presidency of the young State of Israel, but even though he felt very honored, he declined the offer because he didn't feel qualified to accept such a position.

At the end of the twentieth century, *Time* magazine voted Einstein the Person of the Century.

One week before his death he signed a letter to the great philosopher Bertrand Russell in which he agreed that his name should go on a manifesto urging all nations to give up nuclear weapons. It is fitting that one of his last acts was to argue, as he had done all his life, for international peace.

Einstein died on April 18, 1955, at age seventy-six of heart failure in Princeton, New Jersey. At his own request, his funeral and his cremation were very private affairs.

Einstein changed the course of history with his theory of relativity and his famous equation $E = mc^2$. His theories called for nothing less than a new physical concept of the universe that revolutionized our understanding of the nature of the universe.

He ranks with Galileo and Newton as someone who revolutionized man's concepts of space, time, matter, energy, and light and gave man a new and much more profound interest in his universe.

He was truly a concerned citizen of the entire world and one of the legendary figures of the twentieth century.

Lady Lindy

Amelia **Earhart**

"Women, like men, should try to do the impossible. And when they fail, their failure should be a challenge to others."

—Amelia Earhart
(1897–1937)

Imagine this: You have a dream to be the first woman to fly solo across the Atlantic Ocean. But this is the 1920s, a time when women are not even supposed to wear pants, much less pilot a plane. So what do you do? Do you give up your dream and conform to society's rules? Or do you follow your dream?

Your name is Amelia Earhart, and you follow your dream! You will be remembered not only as an important figure in aviation history but also as one of the world's great feminists—a role model for other women who want to accomplish things that no woman has done before.

Amelia was born on July 24, 1897, in Atchison, Kansas, the older of two daughters. Her mother had been the first woman to climb to the top of Pike's Peak in Colorado, and her father had worked his way through law school by shining shoes, building furnace fires, and tutoring other students.

Amelia was a tomboy from the very beginning. She never played with dolls and preferred the sports and games that boys played. Even when she read books, she preferred the adventure stories in which boys did exciting things. She never saw any reason not to do the same things boys did.

Her younger sister Muriel used to say that nothing scared Amelia. Amelia loved the feeling of speed, whether it was galloping on horseback or shooting down their homemade roller coaster.

In high school she was an excellent student, but she was known as a loner who fought for unpopular causes. She didn't attend her graduation, and the school yearbook described her as "the girl in brown who walks alone."[33]

While visiting her sister Muriel who was attending a private school in Canada in 1917, World War I was in full swing, and Amelia decided to help the war effort. She signed on as a volunteer at a military hospital. There she met the Royal Flying Corps and was thrilled by the stories the pilots told.

After the war, she took a course in engine mechanics which was an unusual subject for a woman to study in those days, but it was a perfect course for anyone interested in airplanes. She also took a medical course at Columbia University.

While visiting her parents in California in 1920, she saw an air show and had a ride in a plane (a tiny Kinner Airster) for ten dollars. It was the most exciting thing she'd ever done and she was thrilled.

Many wartime pilots were trying to earn a living in the air and they gave lessons and performed stunts. Amelia wanted to take flying lessons, so she took a job in the mailroom of a telephone company to pay for her lessons.

Less than a year later in June 1921, she made her first solo flight. She continued to work hard and save money, and on her twenty-fifth birthday, she bought a small, bright yellow plane for two thousand dollars which she called the *Canary*.

In 1922 she set her first record, the women's altitude record. She flew higher than any woman had done before— 14,000 feet. She also took to barnstorming at air shows— flying upside down and doing other stunts.

But she could not make a living this way, so she became a social worker at Denison House, Boston's second oldest settlement house. She flew planes in her spare time and became well known as a skilled pilot.

She even began dressing like a flier—in boots, khaki pants, leather jacket, helmet, and goggles.

But flying was still largely a man's world. Another female pilot named Amy Phipps Guest, a wealthy woman, inspired by the daring nonstop solo flight of Charles Lindbergh across the Atlantic in 1927, planned a similar flight herself. She wanted to be the first woman to fly the Atlantic. When her family persuaded her against it, she asked Amelia to take her place.

Amelia was the captain of the flight, but since she lacked the actual flying experience, the actual flying was done by pilot Bill Stultz. Although she would not be at the controls, she would still be in charge of the flight, having the final say on any matter that came up.

She knew how dangerous the flight would be, and she wrote notes to her family to be opened in the event of her death, telling them that even if she lost, the adventure itself was still worthwhile.

On June 17, 1928, Amelia, Bill Stultz, and mechanic Lou Gordon took off from Newfoundland in the *Friendship*. After twenty hours and forty minutes, they arrived safely in Wales.

She had become the first woman passenger to fly across the Atlantic Ocean.

After the *Friendship* flight, she wrote and lectured about flying, competed in the Women's Air Derby, and helped start a new airline. But what she really wanted to do was to fly across the Atlantic by herself.

In 1930 she set the women's speed record of 181 miles per hour, all the while still yearning to fulfill her dream of flying solo across the Atlantic.

When she married George Putnam, a publisher, in 1931, she told him about her dream and he encouraged her.

Amelia began preparing for her flight. She made the necessary repairs on her Lockheed Vega monoplane and practiced "flying blind" until she knew she could handle the plane on instruments alone. Finally on May 21, 1932, she took off from Harbour Grace, Newfoundland, on her historic solo flight.

During the flight, her instruments malfunctioned and she was forced to fly through fog and darkness without knowing her distance from the ocean. As she ran into a storm and was pelted by rain and wind, more parts of the Lockheed Vega failed, but she kept steady on her course and brought the plane safely down in Ireland. She had made it across the Atlantic in slightly less than fifteen hours, the first woman to fly solo across the Atlantic Ocean.

Fame and fortune quickly followed, and besides meeting with foreign dignitaries in London, Paris, and Rome, she was also invited to the White House to meet President Herbert Hoover.

She got a new plane, the twin-engine Lockheed Electra, in 1935, and decided to try what was then aviation's greatest challenge, a flight around the world along the equator. It had been done before, but never by a woman, and always just north of the equator and never at the equator, its widest point.

Amelia and George prepared for months. They studied maps and weather patterns, and finally on June 1, 1937, all was ready. Amelia and her navigator, Fred Noonan, a commercial pilot and navigator, took off.

On July 2, the Electra left New Guinea, heading toward Howland Island.

During the longest and most dangerous part of the trip—a 2,556 mile stretch from New Guinea to Howland Island—the plane was lost. Earhart and Noonan disappeared and no trace of their bodies or the plane was ever found.

We know that she was running low on fuel but we may never know the exact circumstances of her disappearance. It may remain one of the biggest mysteries of the twentieth century.

The words she wrote to her father many years earlier, before her flight on the *Friendship*, serve as her epitaph:

Hooray for the last grand adventure!
I wish I had won, but it was worthwhile anyway.[34]

Newspapers called her Lady Lindy because, dressed in her flying garb, she looked so much like Charles Lindbergh.

She had founded the Ninety-Nines, a women's flying club, and had written three books about flying. One of her most famous books was called *The Fun of It*.

Missing since July 2, 1937, she was legally declared dead January 5, 1939. So far the mystery of her disappearance has never been solved, but recently new clues have surfaced that suggest Amelia and her navigator Fred Noonan possibly landed and eventually died as castaways on Nikumaroro, an uninhabited island in the South Pacific. The island was some three hundred miles southeast of their target destination, Howland Island. The next step in the investigation will be to see if the DNA (known as "touch" DNA) from the recovered objects matches the Earhart reference sample now held by the DNA lab.[35]

Regardless of the results of the investigation, however, the mystery of her death is not as important as her life. The first woman to fly solo across the Atlantic Ocean, she was a pioneer of women's rights, believing that women could do anything they set their minds to.

Mother of the World

Margaret **Mead**

"Never doubt that a group of thoughtful, committed citizens can change the world."

—Margaret Mead
(1901–1978)

Imagine this: You are a twenty-four-year-old woman traveling nine thousand miles to American Samoa all by yourself to study Samoan culture. It is the 1920s, and most people are shocked at the idea of a young woman taking such a trip.

Your name is Margaret Mead, and the trip to Samoa to study Polynesian culture is just the first of many trips you will take to study various cultures around the world. You are a pioneer in your field, and you become the most famous anthropologist in the world.

Margaret was born December 16, 1901, in Philadelphia, Pennsylvania, the oldest of five children. Her father was a professor in the Wharton School of Finance and Commerce, her mother was a sociologist and an early advocate of women's rights, and her paternal grandmother was a pioneer in child psychology.

For the first few years of her life, she was taught at home by her paternal grandmother, Martha Ramsey, a pioneer in child psychology.

Her grandmother had attended college when fewer than 2 percent of Americans did so, and Margaret once said that her grandmother was one of the most important influences in her life.

Grandma Mead didn't think children should have to sit still for more than an hour, and she disapproved of their having to memorize lists of facts. Instead, she sent Margaret outdoors to bring her examples of the plants she had described in their lesson.

Margaret's mother, Emily Fogg Mead, was a sociologist and was also an important influence. Her mother encouraged her to become her own person and reminded her that you had to work hard to turn a gift into an accomplishment.

It was Grandma Mead, however, who first encouraged Margaret to think like an anthropologist. She told her to take notes on the behavior of her two younger sisters, Elizabeth and Priscilla.

Margaret jotted down many of the things her sisters said and did. She didn't know it then, but she had already begun her life as an anthropologist—someone who studies the physical, social, and cultural lives of human beings.

The family moved a great deal, and by the time Margaret was a teenager, the Mead family had lived in sixty different houses.

Being able to feel at home quickly in a new place was a skill that would prove to be a great advantage in later years as she traveled for her work.

She graduated Phi Beta Kappa, an academic honor society from Barnard College in 1923 with a major in psychology. It was at Barnard that she confirmed her interest in anthropology.

After completing her coursework for her doctorate in anthropology at Columbia University, Margaret traveled nine thousand miles to American Samoa, an island east of Australia in the South Seas, to do her first fieldwork, focusing on adolescent girls.

Back then most people were shocked by the idea of a twenty-four-year-old woman taking such a trip, but her family was proud of her.

She arrived at Pago Pago in the fall of 1925. Once there, she tried to blend in with native life while at the same time recording her observations.

She learned the native language (one of seven she eventually mastered) and lived in a Samoan household along with the girls. She found that young Samoan girls experience none of the tensions American and European adolescents suffer from and wrote about the kinds of social arrangements that made this easy transition to adulthood possible.

She spent almost a year in a village on the island of Tau studying the lives of young girls between the ages of twelve and nineteen. She concluded that culture influences personality more than genetics. This and her other findings became the subject of her best-selling book, *Coming of Age in Samoa*, which has been translated into many languages and went on to become the best-selling anthropology book of all time.

Her book presented to the public for the first time the idea that developmental stages could be shaped by cultural demands and expectations which meant that adolescent stages and problems would be different in different cultures.

Her next venture was her trip to New Guinea where she

studied sex roles in culture. She studied the play and imaginations of younger children and the way these children were shaped by adult society. She wanted to learn about children through their drawings, so she took along a thousand sheets of paper which were used in the first month. By the time she left New Guinea, she had almost thirty-five thousand drawings.

She intended to disprove the current theory that the masculine and feminine roles were innate and unchangeable and again concluded that cultural influences were more important than genetic influences.

In Bali she pioneered the use of still photographs (taking more than thirty thousand photographs of the Balinese) and motion picture film for anthropological research.

In each new place she tried to learn the language and understand the culture of the people she was studying. By doing this, she was developing a method of inquiry using observations, interviews, and photographs that other anthropologists could use.

She continued her pioneering anthropological work for the next several decades and wrote more books describing what she had seen and learned.

As time passed, she made fewer field trips to countries where there was no running water or electricity and spent more time teaching anthropology at Columbia University. In 1969 *Time* magazine named her Mother of the World.

A prolific writer, she wrote or co-authored forty-four books and more than one thousand articles that all contributed to the better understanding of people around the world.

She was passionate about what she believed the Western world could learn from developing societies, and in 1944 she established the Institute for Intercultural Studies (now closed as of December 31, 2009).

She had come a long way from the little girl who made observations about her sisters. Her insights into the human family and its relationship to the world encouraged people to focus on the similarities they shared rather than the differences that divided them.

She was the first anthropologist to look at human development from a cross-cultural perspective and had demonstrated that gender roles differed from one society to another and depended at least as much (if not more) on culture as on biology. Through her best-selling books she brought anthropology to ordinary people for the first time.

She hoped that one day people might bring up children who could be at home anywhere in the world—in any kind of house, eating any kind of food, and learning new languages as needed.

She took a particular interest in world hunger and helped establish UNESCO (the United Nations agency committed to establishing world peace through cultural exchange).

She died on November 15, 1978, at age seventy-six from pancreatic cancer, the same cancer that had killed her brother.

When she died, she was the most famous anthropologist in the world and was awarded the Presidential Medal of Freedom posthumously in 1979, America's highest civilian honor.

She believed that cultural patterns of racism, warfare, and environmental exploitation were **learned** and that, therefore, it was possible for members of a society to work together to change things for the better.

Not only was she a renowned anthropologist, but she was also a strong proponent of women's rights and set a colorful example for future generations of women to follow.

In his book *Margaret Mead and Samoa: The Making and Unmaking of an Anthropological Myth*, Australian professor

Derek Freeman was deeply critical of Margret's research,[36] but subsequent reevaluations by other researchers have confirmed most of her findings.

Regardless of the controversy, however, there is still no doubt that she was a major anthropological influence on the twentieth century.

The Lady of Philadelphia

Marian **Anderson**

"I have a great belief in the future of my people and my country."

—Marian Anderson
(1897–1993)

Imagine this: You are a young black woman with a magnificent voice, but you have no money for singing lessons, and even if you could take singing lessons, where would you sing? As a young black woman, many restaurants refuse to serve you and some hotels refuse to give you a room. So where would you sing? Certainly not in any American concert hall.

Your name is Marian Anderson, and with the help of your church and some remarkable people in your life, you do manage to take music lessons. You begin your career singing in Europe, but by the time your career is winding down, you are singing all over the world and you are considered one of the greatest classical singers of all time.

Marian was born in South Philadelphia on February 27, 1897, the first of three daughters.

Her mother had been a teacher and her father sold coal and ice. Her father was also an usher in the church the family attended, and Marian joined the junior choir when she was six.

Mr. Robinson, the choir director, encouraged Marian's musical talent, and when she was eight she talked her father into buying an old piano. There was no money for music lessons, so Marian taught herself enough to play music to sing to.

Following her father's death when she was ten, the family moved in with her paternal grandparents. Her mother supported the family by taking in laundry and working as a cleaning woman, the only kind of work available to black women.

Marian's mother was just the first of several women role models who influenced her immensely. Her mother's faith instilled a core of stability which lasted her entire life.

Music and church were always an important part of Marian's life. By age thirteen she was the youngest member of the senior choir at her church where she thrilled audiences with the three-octave range of her voice.

As she continued to sing, she found another role model who influenced her life. Mary Saunders Patterson was a black music teacher whom Marian met when she was a junior in high school. Ms. Patterson gave her free music lessons and once loaned her a dress to wear to a concert.

Marian learned how to project her voice to the far corner of a room, to enunciate the words to a song clearly, and to strengthen her voice through special exercises.

A third influence was a white woman, Dr. Lucy Wilson, principal of South Philadelphia High School for Girls. Dr.

Wilson rescued Marian from the business courses she was taking to become a secretary, so that she could have more musical training as part of her high school curriculum. Dr. Wilson also arranged for many opportunities for Marian to sing in public.

After graduation from high school, Marian tried to register at a music school in Philadelphia, but the receptionist there told her, "We don't take colored." That music school no longer exists in Philadelphia, but the rejection hurt her deeply.[37]

Dr. Wilson again came to her rescue and arranged for her to audition for Guiseppe Boghetti, a much-sought-after music teacher. When he heard Marian sing "Deep River," he was moved to tears.

With the help of her church and Dr. Wilson arranging benefit concerts for her to raise money, she was able to take private lessons with Boghetti who taught her how to control her breathing and to sing opera.

In 1925 she won an important singing contest in New York City with over three hundred contestants, which resulted in her singing with the New York Philharmonic Orchestra at Lewisohn Stadium.

As a result of that performance, a top concert manager offered to represent her, and she was finally able to support her mother. Marian always said that the greatest moment in her life was the day she told her mother that she could quit her cleaning job in a downtown department store.

Like many other artists both black and white, she had to build a reputation in Europe before American audiences would even consider giving her a chance at the top. And even then she could not escape the racism so deeply embedded in American life. For almost a decade until 1935, her primary musical audiences were European.

In Europe there was no discrimination because of race, and

she was accepted immediately. The Europeans loved her, and she sang before kings and queens.

She returned to the United States in the fall of 1930 and was awarded a fellowship to study in Germany. While studying in Germany, her first concert was so successful that she received invitations to sing in Norway, Sweden, and Denmark.

Although she returned to America for family visits, she always returned to Europe. In America, she was not being booked into the large concert halls, whereas in Europe she was accepted with no problem and performed all over Scandinavia as well as in London, Paris, and Vienna.

While in Europe, she met Sol Hurok, a famous American concert manager, who asked if he could represent her in America, so she returned home once again.

While touring America, she encountered a good deal of discrimination. Some restaurants refused to serve her, and some hotels refused to give her a room.

The most famous case of discrimination in Marian's career occurred in 1939 when the Daughters of the American Revolution refused to let her sing in Constitution Hall in Washington, DC, because she was black. The members of the D.A.R. were descendants of the men who had fought against the British in the American Revolution, but they would not grant a black woman the freedom to perform in their hall.

Many people, including Eleanor Roosevelt, were outraged at this discrimination. Mrs. Roosevelt resigned her membership in the organization and invited Marian to sing instead at an open-air concert Easter Sunday, 1939, on the steps of the Lincoln Memorial in Washington, DC.[38]

Seventy-five thousand people came to see and hear her. They wanted her to know that they didn't approve of the cruel treatment she had received, and millions of people listened to her on the radio. She gave such a great performance that this concert became one of the most famous concerts ever given in the United States.

Her triumphant concert and all the unpleasantness leading up to it were an important episode in the history of race relations in the United States.

Marian began to insist that blacks in her segregated audiences be offered seats equally as good as the seats for the whites. And she demanded that blacks be able to buy tickets on a first-come, first-served basis and not have to wait until whites had been given first choice of the tickets. Eventually, she refused to sing in any concert hall that was segregated.

In 1954 Rudolf Bing, the general manager of the Metropolitan Opera in New York, invited her to sing at the Metropolitan. January 7, 1955, was a historic occasion. Marian was the first black singer to sing with the Metropolitan Opera and at the end of her performance, the audience thundered her name.

In 1963 she received the Presidential Medal of Freedom, America's highest civilian honor, and ten years later she was elected to the National Women's Hall of Fame.

She continued to sing in concerts and operas all over the world until 1965 when she announced her retirement. When she finished her last concert at Carnegie Hall, the audience applauded with such enthusiasm that she sang an extra hour.

After that, she performed only occasionally until her death from congestive heart failure on April 8, 1993, at age ninety-six. More than two thousand admirers attended a memorial service for her at Carnegie Hall in New York City.

Marian Anderson, "The Lady of Philadelphia" and world-leading concert contralto, traveled hundreds of thousands of miles around the world and gave more than a thousand performances during her career.

Perhaps her greatest legacy to the American people, however, was demonstrating by her own example that talent, dignity, and courage were more important than skin color, and that by leading by example one could be an instrument for social change.

Segregation was just ending as Marian Anderson retired, and she had helped to blaze a trail for equal rights in America and open doors for a whole generation of African Americans. She prepared the way for all the young black singers of classical music who came after her.

Trailblazing Photographer

Margaret **Bourke-White**

"Work is something you can count on, a trusted life-long friend who never deserts you."

—Margaret Bourke-White
(1904–1971)

Imagine this: You are an adventurous young woman, and you want to do all those things that women never do. Your passion is photography, but this is a man's field in a man's world, and you are not a man. So what do you do?

Your name is Margaret Bourke-White, and you become the first female war correspondent and the first woman to be allowed to work in combat zones during World War II. You become one of the most important photographers of the twentieth century, and you do, in fact, end up attaining your dream of doing a man's job in a man's world!

Margaret was born in the Bronx, New York, on June 14, 1904, the second of three children. Her father, Joseph White, was an inventor and an engineer, and her mother, Minnie Bourke, was a forward-thinking and loving mother.

In keeping with their religious philosophy, the Whites created a mentally stimulating and moral home in which to raise their children. They encouraged their children to read books, study nature, and think for themselves. In fact, one night the whole family stayed up to watch a butterfly slowly emerge from the chrysalis.

As a child, Margaret was shy and serious and, unlike her classmates, she loved bugs and snakes. One day, she took her pet snakes to school and caused such a panic in the school that the principal forbade her from bringing them ever again.

In addition to being a mechanical engineer and an inventor, her father was an amateur photographer in his spare time, and the White home was filled with his photographs. Margaret often followed her father around the house pretending to take photographs with an empty cigar box, and she helped him develop his prints in the bathtub.

On Sundays he took her on trips to factories. He told her that the beauty of machines was as great as that of nature and that their beauty was in their usefulness to humans.

Once he took her to a foundry where workers melted metal and poured it into molds. She never forgot the power and beauty of that scene with its fiery colors and wished that she could share it with others.

She loved nature as much as her parents and dreamed of one day being a scientist, perhaps a herpetologist (an expert on reptiles and amphibians). She even thought she might some day go into the jungle and bring back animals for natural history museums. She told herself she would do all the things that women never do.

While at the University of Michigan she married an engineering graduate student, but the marriage didn't work out.

She then enrolled at Cornell University in Ithaca, New York, where she took up photography.

After graduating in 1927, she returned to Cleveland, Ohio, where her family was living and opened her own photography studio in a one-room apartment, specializing in architectural photography. She set up her stack of developing trays near the kitchen sink, did her printing in a tiny breakfast alcove, and rinsed photos in the bathtub.

The money she made from shooting elegant homes and gardens by day was spent on photographing steel mills at night and on the weekends.

Her adventurous nature and her dedication to her craft led to her becoming a world-famous photographer by age twenty-five. She took great risks whenever necessary to get just the picture she wanted.

She often climbed high scaffolds, exposed herself to extreme temperatures, and set up her camera in dangerous places to take her photos. She was determined to get the pictures no one else did.

She gained great success photographing for architects and landscape artists, which brought her to the attention of Cleveland's biggest industrial tycoons.

The industrial pictures she took to be used in the book *The Story of Steel* created a sensation, making her famous almost overnight. At the same time, *House and Garden* magazine began publishing some of her landscape photos, and orders began pouring in from industrialists, estate owners, architectural firms, and advertising agencies.

In the spring of 1929 she was recruited by Henry R. Luce as staff photographer for *Fortune* magazine, which was a new business magazine that would make use of dramatic industrial photographs.

The first lead story was to feature Swift & Co., a hog processing plant. She worked with Parker Lloyd-Smith, her editor, until he became too sick from the stench to continue. After she finished photographing the hogs, she left most of her camera equipment behind to be burned.[39] Her documentation of the activity at a hog processing plant was a major step in the development of the photo essay.

In 1930 she made a trip to Russia, becoming the first Western photographer allowed into that country. For five weeks she traveled all over Russia capturing dams, factories, farms, and their workers. She took nearly three thousand photographs; in 1931 she published her book *Eyes on Russia*.

In 1936 Luce hired her as one of the four photojournalists for his new pictorial magazine *Life*. She was the only woman and the only one of the photographers to use her big, heavy camera with tripod instead of the newer, smaller 35-millimeter cameras.

A new way of thinking about her photographs was emerging. Looking beyond patterns and shapes that she could record on film, she now sought to capture emotion.

She made history with the publication of her haunting photos of the Depression in the book *You Have Seen Their Faces*, a collaboration with the best-selling novelist Erskine Caldwell whom she married in 1939 and divorced in 1942.

In early 1941 tensions were running high in Europe, and *Life* asked her to return to Russia to make a comparison between the current Russia and the one that she had seen ten years before when she had traveled there on her own.

She and Caldwell entered Russia through China, and on July 22 they were there when the first bombs fell on Moscow. She was the only foreign photographer present, and the resulting pictures were a major scoop for both her and for *Life*.

She was a war correspondent for the next four years—the

first female war correspondent, the first woman to be allowed to work in combat zones during World War II, and one of the first photographers to enter and document the death camps.

She recorded events from the air, on the battlefield, and as the war wound down, she was one of the first photographers to record the horrors and atrocities of the concentration camp at Buchenwald.

While serving as a war correspondent, she survived a torpedo attack while on a ship to North Africa, and she flew in American bombers on their bombing raids, taking serial pictures of the destruction.

She had become a trailblazing photographer who photographed the major events of the day. She showed Americans the beauty of industry and its machinery in the 1920s, documented poverty and suffering during the Great Depression in the 1930s, and brought home World War II in the 1940s.

Her assignments took her around the world, and she is probably best remembered for her work for *Life*. One of the magazine's original photographers, she helped develop the photo-essay style of news reporting that proved so popular with readers across the nation.

At one point in her life, a rumor had spread that she was really a man using a woman's name to get extra publicity because of some of the daring feats her photographs required. To document that she was indeed a woman, she had her assistant photograph her while she was actually taking some of her more daring photographs.

She died on August 27, 1971, at age sixty-seven after spending the last seventeen years of her life fighting her Parkinson disease (a degenerative illness which attacks the nervous system) with the same bravery and determination that had made her a great photographer.

They Stood Alone*!*

She was a woman doing a man's job in a man's world, from the foundries of Cleveland to the battlefields of World War II.

She was an original staff photographer for two of the most prominent magazines of her day, *Fortune* and *Life*, and she led a life full of adventure, pioneering a new art form: photojournalism. She was, and still is, one of the most important photographers of the twentieth century.

Pioneer of the Modern Environmental Movement

Rachel **Carson**

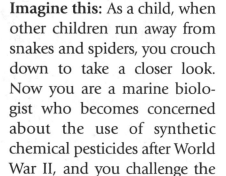

"Most of us walk unseeing through the world."

—Rachel Carson
(1907–1964)

Imagine this: As a child, when other children run away from snakes and spiders, you crouch down to take a closer look. Now you are a marine biologist who becomes concerned about the use of synthetic chemical pesticides after World War II, and you challenge the practices of the agricultural scientists and the government. You call for a change in the way we view the natural world.

Your name is Rachel Carson, and your work starts a worldwide environmental revolution. Your book *Silent Spring* reveals the damage that chemical pesticides such as DDT are doing to our environment and helps set the stage for the US environmental movement of the late twentieth century.

Rachel was born May 27, 1907, the youngest of three children in Springdale, Pennsylvania, where she grew up in a tiny wooden house with no electricity, heat, or plumbing on sixty-five acres of land.

Her mother, Maria McLean Carson, a former school teacher, was an avid reader and shared her knowledge of natural history, botany, and birds, but even more importantly she passed on to Rachel a deep appreciation of the beauty and mystery of the natural world and a lifelong love of nature and all living things.

Not only did Rachel's mother put spiders and other insects out of the house rather than kill them, but also insisted that when her children returned from their woodland adventures with treasures to show her, that they always return the treasures to where they had found them.

From the very beginning Rachel shared her mother's love of nature, and even as a small child, she could recognize a bird by its song and name the different fish in the stream.

She later said, "I can remember no time when I wasn't interested in the out-of-doors and the whole world of nature."[40]

Anna Comstock's popular *Handbook of Nature Study* had brought the nature study movement into the home and classroom, and Maria Carson was the perfect nature-study teacher.

While Rachel's brother and sister were in school, she and her mother spent their time outdoors walking the woods and orchards, exploring the springs, and naming the flowers, birds, and insects. And at night she and her mother hunted for spiders working on webs or moths that ventured out while birds slept.

Rachel's mother encouraged her to use her imagination, and one of Rachel's artistic ventures was a little book of animals she drew and colored herself. The book reflected the strong relationship that existed between the child author and the wild creatures pictured in her book. She identified all the woodland creatures as her friends.

Her mother had great respect for the written word and read to her children nearly every evening. Rachel also loved to read, and her romantic view of nature was influenced by the children's magazines to which her mother subscribed.

Rachel began submitting stories and essays to her favorite magazine, *St. Nicholas*, which had also adopted the values of the nature study movement.

As more and more of Rachel's work was published, her mother encouraged her literary talent and intellectual development and encouraged her to set academic goals for herself.

Her mother remained her best friend and strongest supporter throughout her life, and later on when Rachel was recognized for her accomplishments both as a scientist and as a writer, she acknowledged that her mother had been the dominant influence in her life.

After her mother's death, Rachel believed her mother resembled Albert Schweitzer in her love of life and all living things.

Because of the family's meager means, school had never been a happy place for Rachel who was teased because of the hand-me-down clothing she wore.

She counted the minutes until she could go home where she could immerse herself in her books, the farm animals, the many dogs, and the outdoors.

But in some ways the Carsons' marginal economic status made it easier for Rachel to be independent since she was under no pressure whatever to conform to the social values of her peers.

By the time she entered high school, she had embraced her

mother's view that intellect and a sense of personal worth were far more important than material possessions or social recognition.

During her last two years of high school, she commuted to a high school across the river where she did make some friends, and where her senior yearbook recognized both her academic skills and her perfectionism.

Determined to be a writer, she entered the Pennsylvania College for Women (now Chatham College), but feeling that she didn't have enough imagination to write fiction, she turned to biology, which always gave her more than enough material for her writing.

She graduated in 1929, then received her master's degree in zoology from Johns Hopkins University in 1932. Limited finances forced her to withdraw from the doctoral program in 1934.

In 1936 she took a job as a writer and marine biologist with the US Bureau of Fisheries (which later became the US Fish and Wildlife Service). Over the next fifteen years she was promoted to staff biologist and editor in chief of all its publications.

Her enthusiasm for nature was matched only by her love of writing and poetry, and her job enabled her to combine both her loves: writing and science.

In 1952 she published her prize-winning book *The Sea Around Us* which told the story of the sea from the earliest times and described everything from the smallest sea creatures to the great underwater mountains in the deepest oceans.

No one had ever told the story of the sea like this, and it won the National Book Award for Nonfiction as well as several other honors. The book remained on the *New York Times* Best Sellers list for eighty-six weeks and was so successful that she was able to retire and become a full-time writer.

Her most important book, *Silent Spring*, published in 1962, was about the use of chemical pesticides, and it changed forever the way people thought about their world. Following four years of research, she had identified the devastating and irrevocable hazards of DDT, one of the most powerful pesticides the world had ever known, and she concluded that DDT should be banned.

Her book caused a firestorm of controversy and helped set the stage for the US environmental movement of the late twentieth century.

Her best-selling book focused public attention on the problem of pesticides and other chemical pollution, and led to such landmark legislation as the US Clean Water Act and the banning of DDT in many countries throughout the world.

DDT was eventually banned in the United States, and many of the ideas we have today about protecting the environment can be traced back to Cranston's book.

During the four years it took for her to complete *Silent Spring*, she was fighting breast cancer and then bone cancer, and she eventually died of cancer April 14, 1964, at the age of fifty-six in her home in Silver Spring, Maryland.

In 1973, nine years after her death, she was inducted into the National Women's Hall of Fame, and in 1980 she was awarded the Presidential Medal of Freedom, America's highest civilian honor.

There is currently some controversy about the banning of DDT because of the rise in malaria deaths. The World Health Organization recently estimated that there are between 300 and 500 million cases of malaria annually, resulting in approximately one million deaths—many whose lives could have been saved with the regular application of DDT to their environments.[41]

Regardless of the controversy, however, Rachel Carson was a pioneering naturalist who has been called the founder of the

US environmental movement. An award-winning scientist and writer, her book *Silent Spring* started a worldwide environmental revolution. By identifying the devastating and irrevocable hazards of DDT, one of the most powerful pesticides the world has known, she showed how changing one small part of nature can upset the balance of the whole.

Her dedication to the beauty and integrity of life continues to inspire new generations to protect the living world and all its creatures.

Saint of the Poor

Mother Teresa

"We can do no great things; only small things with great love."

—Mother Teresa
(1910–1997)

Imagine this: At the age of twelve you receive a call from God to become a nun and serve the poor. At age seventeen you make your final decision to become a nun and you do go to India. Then in 1946 you receive your second call from God—to leave the convent and live among the poorest of the poor.

Your name is Sister Teresa, and you exchange your nun's habit for a white cotton sari like those worn by poor women in India. You devote your life to serving the poor on the streets of Calcutta, and in 1950 the pope gives you permission to set up a new order of nuns, the Missionaries of Charity. As head of the new order, you now become known as Mother Teresa, and your ministry spreads to countries all over the world. In 1979 you are awarded one of the most prestigious awards of all, the Nobel Peace Prize.

Agnes Gonxha Bojaxhiu was born in Skopje, a city situated at the crossroads of the Balkans, August 26, 1910, the youngest of three children. At home she was called Gonxha, which in Albanian means a flower bud, because she was plump and cheerful.

Her father Nikola was a wealthy merchant and also a public-spirited man who gave generously to the church, fed the poor at his own table, and set an example of service to the community. He valued family, hard work, and faith above all else and no one in need was ever turned away. This was a lesson that Agnes never forgot.

Her father died when she was eight, and, although the family was no longer wealthy, Agnes's mother, Drane, still continued her husband's generous ways, giving food and help to the poor and the old. The power of this example of practical Christianity stayed with Agnes throughout her life.

After her father's death, Agnes grew even closer to her mother, and they spent as much time in church as at home. Her mother was a deeply religious woman, and Agnes often accompanied her into the town's poorest neighborhoods where they gave out food, medicine, clothes, and money to the poor.

Sometimes the mother-daughter pair cared for a sick widow who couldn't look after her six children. On other days they tended an elderly woman named File who lived alone and had no one to see to her needs. Drane told Agnes that serving the poor was a way to serve God.

At Sunday school Agnes listened attentively to talks about

the priests and nuns working among the people, especially the children, in India. One day when she was twelve, she was praying when she felt a call from God deep inside her to become a nun and work in India.

Moved by the photographs of starving families in India, she made her final decision at age seventeen to become a nun and go to India.

At age eighteen, she applied to join the Loreto Order (an international order of nuns) in India, but first she had to travel to the Loreto Abbey in Ireland to learn English. When she boarded the train for Ireland, it was the last time she would ever see her mother.

After just two months in Ireland, she was sent to the Loreto House in Darjeeling, India, to begin her novitiate, the first step toward taking her final vows as a nun. For the next two years she learned to live as a nun, and she also studied English and Bengali, one of the Indian languages.

At age twenty-one, she completed her novitiate training and took the name Teresa after Therese of Lisieux, a French nun who believed in the little way—working for good by carrying out very simple tasks joyfully.

She was sent to teach geography and history at St. Mary's, a Loreto school in Calcutta. She loved her work, and in 1937 she became principal of the school and took her final vows as a Loreto nun.

After nine happy years in the Loreto order, her life changed very dramatically on September 10, 1946, a day she later remembered as her "Day of Inspiration." She received her second call from God—what she called "a call within her call"—to leave the convent and serve the poor while living among them. She was called to serve the poorest of the poor.[42]

In 1948 the Vatican granted Sister Teresa permission to

leave the Sisters of Loreto and to work with the poor on the streets of Calcutta.

She exchanged her nun's habit for a white cotton sari like those worn by the poor women in India. The sari had a blue border to remind her of the Virgin Mary, and she wore this uniform for the rest of her life.

After a short course in nursing she went out for the first time by herself to work in the slums of Calcutta. She had just five rupees in her pocket and she began by starting a school on the street.

In her simple white sari, Sister Teresa soon became a familiar sight in the slums of Calcutta. She shared the slum dwellers' meager existence and diet, often only rice and salt.

In addition to running her school, she set out on foot each day to distribute food and medicines. Hunger and disease were everywhere. She found old or sick people left on the streets to die, eaten by rats and insects. And unwanted babies were thrown onto piles of garbage.

Soon she was joined by other women who wanted to help the poor of Calcutta, and on October 7, 1950, the Pope gave Sister Teresa permission to set up a new order of nuns, the Missionaries of Charity. As head of the new order, Sister Teresa now became known as Mother Teresa.

In addition to their vows of poverty, chastity, and obedience, the Missionaries of Charity added a new vow: "to give wholehearted, free service to the poorest of the poor." This fourth vow is what set them apart from the other orders.

In 1953, as more and more women came to join them, the Missionaries of Charity moved to a larger house called the Motherhouse.

The nuns led very simple lives. Each nun owned only three saris, a pair of sandals, underwear, a crucifix, a bucket to wash in, and a prayer book. They woke before five o'clock in the morning to pray before going out to work in the slums all day.

In addition to feeding the poor and tending the sick, they also set up homes for the very sick people dying alone on the streets, to give them a place to die with dignity.

But Mother Teresa wanted to help the poor to live as well as to die, so they opened more schools, rescued unwanted babies, and set up homes for abandoned or orphaned slum children. They also set up centers to help people suffering from leprosy, a disease that deforms the body.

After the success of her mission in Calcutta, Mother Teresa went to Venezuela in South America to open her first mission outside India in 1965. Since then her work has expanded to include more than 600 missions in 136 countries.

In 1979 she was awarded one of the most prestigious prizes of all, the Nobel Peace Prize. She accepted the award in the name of the poor and used the money to feed the poor and build more homes for the homeless and people suffering from leprosy.

Mother Teresa had personally succeeded in bridging the gulf between rich nations and poor nations. Some people called her the most powerful woman in the world because when she called, prime ministers and presidents around the world responded.

She was always concerned about the poverty of the spirit as well as the poverty of the body, and she often talked about living in a throw-away society, where people as well as things were rejected and thrown away.

Love was the primary message of her ministry and she urged people to love until it hurts. She often said that "being unwanted is the worst disease that any human being can ever experience."

When she was nearly eighty years old, she began to suffer from heart trouble, and in 1990 she resigned as the head of the Missionaries of Charity because of poor health. Although she became increasingly weak, she continued to travel and to work at the Home for the Destitute and Dying in Calcutta.

Finally in March 1997 she became too frail to carry on and she died of a heart attack on September 5, 1997, at the Motherhouse. Nearly one-half million people of all religions— ordinary people as well as world leaders—came to say a final good-bye to her.

Today, the small wooden board outside the door to the Motherhouse reads, *Mother Teresa*. In honor of her life and her dedication to the poor, the IN and OUT indicator is fixed because Mother is always IN.

The Mother of the Modern Day Civil Rights Movement

Rosa **Parks**

★

"The only tired I was,
was tired of giving in."
—Rosa Parks
(1913–2005)

Imagine this: It's December 1, 1955, and you're a forty-two-year-old black woman taking the bus home after work. It's been a long day and you're very tired. You sit in the first seat for blacks which is right behind the white section. After a few stops, a white man gets on the bus and looks for an empty seat, but there aren't any. Then the bus driver comes over to you and asks you to give up your seat to the white man. In the past, you've done this many times, but what are you going to do tonight? Are you going to give up your seat or are you going to refuse to move?

Your name is Rosa Parks, and you refuse to move. Your refusal to give up your seat that night leads to a bus boycott by black people that lasts over a year, and the Montgomery bus boycott helps launch the civil rights movement which leads to President Lyndon B. Johnson signing the Civil Rights Act in 1964.

Rosa was born February 4, 1913, in Tuskegee, Alabama, the first of two children, and she was born the same year that Harriet Tubman died. Her father was a carpenter, and her mother had once been a teacher.

Growing up in Montgomery, Alabama, she hated the unfair rules that black people had to live by. Black children could not attend the same schools as white children. Black families could not eat in white restaurants or use white swimming pools or see movies at white theaters. And they could only use restrooms and drinking fountains with signs that said "Colored Only."

While her father was working in the North, she lived with her mother, grandparents, and younger brother on the grandparents' farm. Her grandparents taught her that all people deserved fair treatment, regardless of their skin color. Rosa was an excellent student and at age eleven she went to a private school for black girls run by a white woman from the North named Alice White who believed that black girls deserved a good education. Unfortunately, it closed down before Rosa could finish high school.

A few weeks before her twentieth birthday, she married Raymond Parks, a barber, who shared many of her values. After their marriage, they moved to Montgomery where, encouraged by Raymond, she received her high school diploma in 1933.

When they moved to Montgomery, they joined the Montgomery chapter of the NAACP (the National Association for the Advancement of Colored People), an organization that worked to help black people gain their civil rights. She was elected its secretary and assisted the chapter's president, Edgar Daniel Nixon.

She also joined the Montgomery Voters League and visited the homes of black people and taught them how to pass the voting test so they could vote.

She refused to ride in the elevators in public buildings that were marked "Colored" and used the stairs instead. And on hot days, even though her throat was dry, she still walked right past the water fountains marked "Colored."

She also often walked the mile to and from work rather than ride the bus because the buses were worst of all. Black people had to get on at the front door and pay their fare, then get off the bus and walk to the back door and board the bus again. Sometimes the driver drove away before the black passengers reached the back door even after they had paid their fares.

If the black person did manage to get on the bus, he was allowed to sit only in the seats at the back of the bus because the seats in the front half were reserved for whites. And if a white person got on the bus and there were no empty seat, the black person sitting closest to the white section was expected to give up his seat to the white person.

On Thursday evening, December 1, 1955, forty-two year-old Rosa Parks left work and started home after a long and tiring day as a seamstress. Her shoulders ached from being hunched over her sewing machine, and she decided to take the bus.

She got on and sat in the first seat for blacks right behind the white section. After a few stops, all the seats were filled when a white man got on. The bus driver told Rosa and the other three black people in her row to give up their seats to the white man because blacks and whites could not sit together in the same row. The other three blacks got up, but Rosa decided it was time to stand up for herself, and she refused to move.

She had paid her fare, and she believed that she was entitled to ride the bus just as much as the white man. After Rosa refused to give up her seat, the bus driver got off the bus and returned with two policemen. Rosa was arrested, photographed, fingerprinted, and placed in a jail cell. She cooperated and remained calm throughout the entire humiliating process.

When Nixon, president of the NAACP, heard the news, he posted her bond so that she could be released. Then he drove her home where they met with her husband and Fred Gray, an attorney, and talked about what had happened. They decided that Mr. Gray would go to court with Rosa on Monday and prove that the bus company was not obeying the United States Constitution.

The next night Rosa met with a group of ministers and other black leaders of the city, and they decided to boycott the buses. They printed up 35,000 flyers telling black people not to ride the buses on Monday, December 5, the day of Rosa's trial. And on Sunday morning black ministers all over the city told their congregations to support Rosa by not riding the buses.

On Monday morning, no blacks were seen anywhere on Montgomery's buses. The few blacks who owned cars organized car pools, some rode bicycles, a few rode mules to their jobs, but most of them walked. And sometimes they sang.

When a black minister stopped his car to ask a frail, elderly black lady if she would prefer to take the bus, she told him, "My feets is weary, but my soul is rested."[43]

At her trial that morning, the judge found Rosa guilty, but Rosa and her attorney appealed the verdict and said they would take their case to a higher court.

Thousands of people attended the church meeting that night where it was decided that the boycott would continue until black people were given fair treatment by the bus company.

Black people refused to ride Montgomery buses for 381 days—more than a year. The newspapers began calling Montgomery "the walking city." The bus company refused to change, so black black people just kept on walking.

Rosa received many threats and some homes were bombed, but she knew they had to continue their protest. After two months, more than a hundred leaders of the protest were arrested, including Rosa. Reporters came to Montgomery from all over the United States and from other countries, and they all wrote stories for their papers about the arrests.

The black citizens of Montgomery walked all year and in all kinds of weather, and the bus company lost thousands of dollars.

On December 20, 1956, the US Supreme Court ruled that the bus company's segregation rules were unconstitutional and therefore illegal. The bus company had no choice but to obey the Supreme Court's ruling against bus segregation.

A year had passed since Rosa Parks had refused to give up her seat on the bus. Now black people could sit in any seat and would not have to give up their seats for anyone.

The bus company was ordered to hire black bus drivers, and, most importantly, black people had learned that they had the power to change things.

Some people called Rosa Parks the Mother of the Civil Rights Movement because people in other places read about Montgomery and began to follow her example.

Rosa Parks changed the lives of African Americans in Montgomery and all across America with one courageous act.

Her refusal to give up her seat on the bus, the yearlong protest that followed it, and the part of the civil rights movement that grew from it all have an important place in the long history of the African American struggle for freedom and justice.

The Montgomery bus boycott helped launch the civil rights movement that led to President Lyndon B. Johnson signing the Civil Rights Act in 1964.

In 1996 President Clinton presented Rosa with the Presidential Medal of Freedom, America's highest civilian honor.

She spent her last years living quietly in Detroit where she died in 2005 at the age of ninety-two. After her death, her casket was placed in the rotunda of the United States Capitol for two days, so the nation could pay its respects to the woman whose courage had changed the lives of so many. She had been proof that the act of one person can change the world.

He Broke the Color Barrier!

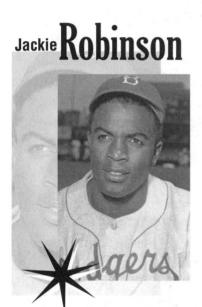

Jackie Robinson

"The first freedom for all people is freedom of choice."

—Jackie Robinson
(1919–1972)

Imagine this: You are a young black man who wants to play professional baseball, but it's 1944 and there are no African Americans playing on any of the major league teams. So what do you do?

Your name is Jackie Robinson, and you join the Kansas City Monarchs, a Negro League team, and refuse to give up your dream to play professional baseball. In 1945 Branch Rickey, general manager of the Brooklyn Dodgers, invites you to join the Montreal Royals, the Dodgers top minor league team because he believes it's time to end segregation in baseball and he thinks you're just the man to do it. On April 15, 1947, when the major league season opens, you are there in the Dodger lineup, the first African American to play baseball for a major league team.

Jackie was born January 31, 1919, in a small farmhouse in Cairo, Georgia, the youngest of five children, the grandson of a slave, and the son of a sharecropper.

When Jackie was only six months old, his father took off for Florida and was never heard from again. Without his father to work the farm, Jackie and his family had to leave the farm.

In 1920 in an effort to escape the discrimination problems of the Deep South, Jackie's mother moved her family to Pasadena, California, where they shared a small apartment with his uncle. His mother took in washing to pay her way, and Jackie often ate day-old-bread dipped in milk and sugar for supper.

Somehow his mother managed to save a little money, and a welfare agency helped her buy a small house. They were the only black family on their street, and the prejudice they encountered only strengthened their family bond.

Some of their white neighbors called the children names and even started a petition to get the family thrown out of the neighborhood, but Jackie's mother stood her ground and refused to let their racial taunts drive her and her family away.

His mother was up before dawn six days a week, spent a full day cleaning other people's houses, and then came home exhausted, but she was always there to try to keep her children on track. She expected them to do well in school, and although Jackie was a good student, his heart was always more into sports and games than in his schoolwork.

After school, he hauled junk, shined shoes, and sold newspapers to make money. He also hung out with a local gang, the Pepper Street gang, and was headed for trouble until two men changed his life.

The first was Carl Anderson, a local mechanic who took an

150

interest in him and convinced him that if he continued with the gang, he would end up hurting his mother as well as himself.

The other man was the pastor of his church, Reverend Carl Downs, who became his friend and counselor and helped channel his energy into sports.

Jackie played all sports and he played them well. He won the city championship the first time he took up table tennis, and he became a four-sport star at his high school—earning letters in football, track, baseball, and basketball.

At Pasadena Junior College in 1938 he set a new broad jump record in the morning, and then in the afternoon he changed into his baseball uniform. Playing shortstop, he helped his team win the league championship.

His football and basketball teams also won league titles, and college coaches rushed to offer him athletic scholarships.

Jackie chose the University of California at Los Angeles (UCLA), which was close to his home. Football was his first love in those days, and he played halfback and safety on UCLA's unbeaten 1939 team.

After the season ended, he moved on to basketball, track, and baseball and became the university's first student to earn varsity letters in four sports.

In the spring of 1941 he quit school because he wanted to begin earning money to help his mother, and he wasn't sure if a college degree would really help a black man get a good job.

On December 7, 1941, the Japanese bombed Pearl Harbor, and six months later Jackie received his draft notice to serve his country.

The army sent him to Fort Riley, Kansas, where he completed his basic training, organized a baseball team, and applied for Officer Candidate School (OCS). But the army was not accepting black officer candidates.

Jackie complained to Joe Louis, the world heavyweight boxing champion, who also happened to be at Fort Riley at the time. Soon after that, Jackie's orders for OCS came through, and he graduated in 1943 as a second lieutenant.

After his discharge from the army in 1944, he wanted to play baseball, but at that time, there were no African Americans playing on any of the major league teams.

He joined the Kansas City Monarchs, a Negro League team where he continued to encounter as much racial discrimination as in the army. Many hotels and restaurants refused to serve black people, so he and his teammates often slept and ate on the bus.

But in New York, one man was planning to break baseball's color barrier. Branch Rickey, owner of the Brooklyn Dodgers, had decided it was time to end segregation in baseball.

Rickey knew that the first black Dodger would be abused by fans and players alike, so the man would have to be more than just a great baseball player. He would have to be an exceptional human being.

In 1945 Rickey decided that Jackie was that man! Rickey gave Jackie examples of insults he might hear and then told him he needed a player "with the guts not to fight back."

Jackie knew it would be hard, but he accepted the challenge because he hoped he could help open doors for all black men everywhere.

Jackie joined the all-white Montreal Royals, the Dodgers' top minor league team and, though taunted by fans, he never lost his cool. Rickey decided it was time to move Jackie up to the major leagues.

April 15, 1947, was a historic day for major league baseball and for the entire nation. When the major league season opened that day, Jackie was there in the Dodger lineup, the first African American to play baseball for a major league team.

In the beginning, his white teammates tried to ignore him, but as the fans and opposing players abused Jackie with cat-calls and racial taunts, his teammates united behind him.

In one incident, while fans harassed Robinson from the stands, Dodgers shortstop and team captain Pee Wee Reese walked over and put his arm around Robinson, a gesture that has become legendary in baseball history.[44]

And in 1950 when the Dodgers were in Cincinnati to play the Reds, there was even a death threat addressed to Jackie and two other players, warning them not to show up for that day's game. Two secret service men were assigned to each of the three athletes, and everyone played.[45]

Jackie rose above the harassment and answered the abuse with his bat and his feet. His .297 batting average helped the Dodgers win the National League pennant. He led the National League in stolen bases and was named Rookie of the Year. Then in 1949 he was named the league's Most Valuable Player (MVP) and also starred in a movie about his life.

In his ten seasons with the Dodgers, they won six National League pennants.

In 1957 he retired from baseball with an impressive career batting average of .311, and in 1962 he was voted into the National Baseball Hall of Fame, the first black man to receive baseball's highest honor. In 1972 the Dodgers retired his uniform number 42.

His courageous example paved the way for the full integration of major league baseball in the years that followed. Over the course of the 1960s, twelve of the sixteen baseball teams had black players, with blacks gaining acceptance into basketball and football as well.

Jackie Robinson's life and legacy will be remembered as one of the most important in American history, and in 1997, the world celebrated the fiftieth anniversary of his breaking the Major League Baseball's color barrier.

Jackie died in 1972 at age fifty-three from heart problems and complications from diabetes. At his funeral, Reverend Jesse Jackson said, "No grave can hold that body down because it belongs to the ages!"[46]

Branch Rickey had chosen well. Jackie Robinson was not only a great ballplayer, but he was also a great human being!

He Walked on the Moon!

Neil **Armstrong**

"That's one small step for man, one giant leap for mankind."

—Neil Armstrong
(1930–)

Imagine this: People have dreamed of reaching the moon for hundreds of years, but no one has ever tried to land a spacecraft there. Now, that may actually be possible, and you want to be the one to do it.

Your name is Neil Armstrong, and it's July 20, 1969. You're 38 years old, and you do, in fact, become the first human being to walk on the moon.

Neil was born August 5, 1930, in Wapakoneta, Ohio, the oldest of three children. Growing up, he loved to read and he read ninety books in the first grade alone.

One Sunday in 1936 six-year-old Neil's life was changed forever. He was supposed to be at church but instead, his father and he sneaked off to the airport where a pilot was in town offering rides in his tri-motor airplane known as the Tin Goose.

After that first plane ride, Neil wanted to fly, and he spent all his free time building model airplanes. He made hundreds of model planes and even built a wind tunnel in his basement so he could test them.

By the time he was nine, he was decorating his bedroom with planes hung from the ceiling, and when he wasn't building model planes, he spent his spare time reading about planes. He especially enjoyed reading about the Wright brothers who had invented the first airplane in 1903.

When he was fifteen, he started taking flying lessons. Each lesson cost nine dollars per hour and he worked at a hardware store, a grocery store, and later a pharmacy to pay for his lessons. He earned forty cents per hour at the pharmacy, so it took him a long time to save up enough money for even one lesson. But soaring through the sky was worth all the hard work.

On his sixteenth birthday, he received the best possible present—his pilot's license. Now he could fly on his own! He had his pilot's license before he earned his driver's license.

In school, he liked science, math, and astronomy and found the planets and stars to be almost as amazing as airplanes. He was particularly fascinated by the moon.

After high school, he wanted to go to college to earn a degree in aeronautical engineering (the study of designing aircraft) and build new kinds of airplanes, but his parents couldn't afford to pay for college. So once again he worked hard to meet his goal. He studied hard, worked odd jobs, and flew whenever he could.

In 1947 the United States Navy offered him a scholarship for study at a school of his choice, so he began work on an aeronautical engineering degree at Purdue University. In return for the scholarship, he agreed to join the Navy after college.

Before he could earn his degree, however, a war started in Korea, and in 1949 he was called to active duty with the Navy. After some brief training, he was assigned to an aircraft, the USS *Essex*, as a fighter pilot. His dream of being a pilot had come true.

He flew seventy-eight missions during the Korean War and received three medals for courage. He became known as a pilot who could handle all kinds of danger.

After his tour of duty was over, he returned to college in 1952 and, to earn money, he delivered newspapers before most students were even awake.

After graduating in 1955, he headed to Edwards Air Force Base in California where the American government was building and testing new kinds of airplanes, just what Neil wanted to do.

His most exciting job there was testing the X-15 rocket plane which was almost like going into space. On one flight in 1962 he reached a peak altitude of 207,500 feet.

In 1957 the Soviet Union launched Sputnik, the first satellite, into space and the Space Age was born. And on April 12, 1961, Soviet Yuri Gagarin became the first human in space when he made one orbit around the Earth.

The United States was determined to catch up, and in 1961 President John F. Kennedy announced his determination to land an American on the moon by 1970.

On February 20, 1962, astronaut John Glenn orbited the Earth three times in the space capsule *Friendship 7*, and Neil decided to apply for NASA's (the National Aeronautics and Space Administration) astronaut program.

Out of hundreds of hopeful pilots, Neil and eight others were chosen in September 1962.

They Stood Alone!

After several years of intensive training, all his hard work paid off, and he was named commander of a mission called *Gemini 8*. He was going into space at last! The goal of *Gemini 8* was to join together two spacecraft in space, an operation known as docking, which had never been attempted before. If successful, docking would be an important part of NASA's plan to reach the moon.

On March 16, 1966, the *Gemini 8* spacecraft was launched with Neil Armstrong and fellow astronaut David Scott. The astronauts flew twice around Earth and then spotted their target: an unmanned rocket that had been launched into space ahead of *Gemini 8*. The two astronauts carefully guided their capsule toward the rocket. They lined the vehicles up and docked them together. Success!

The mission had to end prematurely because of mechanical problems with the spacecraft, but Neil and his copilot David Scott had proved that spacecraft could be docked.

In January 1969 NASA named Neil commander of *Apollo 11*. For the first time, human beings would try to land on the moon, and Neil would be their leader.

For six months he trained harder than he ever had, spending up to fourteen hours a day practicing on simulators.

On July 16, 1969, the crew of *Apollo* (Neil, Michael Collins, and Buzz Aldrin) entered their capsule while an estimated 528 million people watched on television as the huge rocket shot into space. After three days of flight, the moon came into view.

The next day, *Apollo 11* split into two spacecraft. Michael Collins stayed behind in the command module, now called *Columbia*. He would orbit the moon while Neil and Buzz headed down to the surface of the moon in the lunar module, now called *Eagle*.

But there was a problem! The planned landing area was

cluttered with rocks the size of cars. *Eagle* could not land safely there.

With just forty seconds of fuel left, Neil spotted a flat, clear patch of ground. Slowly, he eased *Eagle* down. They were on the moon! After landing safely, he radioed back to Earth, "The *Eagle* has landed."[47]

The astronauts put on their heavy space suits, helmets, gloves, and boots. They knew the world would be watching. Television cameras on *Eagle* recorded every movement and beamed the images back to Earth. He could see his footprints in the fine sandy particles on the moon. The world waited to hear Neil's first words: "That's one small step for man . . . one giant leap for mankind."[48]

The two astronauts collected samples of rocks and soil for scientists to study and they left behind the American flag, their footprints, and a plaque. Along with their signatures, the plaque carried a message for future visitors which included the words: "We came in peace for all Mankind."[49]

Neil and Buzz spent the night safely inside the spacecraft. Then Neil fired up the engine and *Eagle* blasted off from the moon. Neil triggered the rocket motor, and *Eagle* separated into two halves—the lower half remaining on the Moon while the other half sped back up toward the *Columbia* where Mike Collins was waiting for them.

Three hours later *Eagle* and *Columbia* docked and after Buzz and Neil joined Mike in *Columbia*, *Eagle* was allowed to fall back to the Moon while *Columbia* started its long journey home.

The *Columbia* splashed down into the Pacific Ocean on July 24, 1969. *Apollo 11* had made exploration history!

After returning home, the three astronauts went on a world tour, and then Neil retired to a more quiet, less public life.

He had received many special awards and honors, including the Presidential Medal of Freedom, the Congressional Space Medal of Honor, the NASA Distinguished Service Medal, and was inducted into the US Astronaut Hall of Fame on March 19, 1993.

The young boy who had dreamed of flying planes had indeed left his mark in the history of space exploration!

a final thought

You have just read about some extraordinary men and women who made unique contributions that changed and shaped the course of history. They were not afraid to take a risk even when it meant standing alone, and by stepping out and away from the crowd, they changed their world.

You have seen that one individual can indeed make a difference!

My hope is that their lives will inspire you to believe in yourself and to soar to new heights of your own.

Although all these people stood alone—at least against the beliefs and expectations of their particular society—I should note that in another sense, no one ever really stands alone. All our lives intertwine to some degree.

Although Copernicus argued against the commonly held Ptolemaic view of the universe, he still relied heavily on Ptolemy's work. Galileo stood on the shoulders of Copernicus, both Copernicus and Galileo influenced Newton, and Newton influenced Einstein. Thoreau influenced Gandhi, and Gandhi's influence was felt by Rosa Parks and the entire civil rights movement in this country. And so on and so on.

We all need role models, so let us choose our role models

carefully. And hopefully we, in turn, may become role models for those who follow us.

I want to leave you with a few suggestions to consider that may influence how you live your life:

Live your own life as only you can live it.
Do what you love and love what you do.
Discover your passion and have the courage
to follow your heart.

Remember, you, too, can make a difference!

**MAY YOU ALWAYS FOLLOW YOUR HEART
AND NEVER GIVE UP YOUR DREAM!**

The Road Not Taken

Two roads diverged in a yellow wood,
And sorry I could not travel both
And be one traveler, long I stood
And looked down one as far as I could
To where it bent in the undergrowth;

Then took the other, as just as fair,
And having perhaps the better claim,
Because it was grassy and wanted wear;
Though as for that the passing there
Had worn them really about the same,

And both that morning equally lay
In leaves no step had trodden black.
Oh, I kept the first for another day!
Yet knowing how way leads on to way,
I doubted if I should ever come back.

I shall be telling this with a sigh
Somewhere ages and ages hence:
Two roads diverged in a wood, and I—
I took the one less traveled by,
And that has made all the difference.

—Robert Frost
(1874–1963)

acknowledgments

Photo credits: Photographs of Christopher Columbus, Leonardo da Vinci, Nicolaus Copernicus, Galileo Galilei, Isaac Newton, Elizabeth Cady Stanton, Henry David Thoreau, Harriet Tubman, Clara Barton, Nikola Tesla, Booker T. Washington, Marie Curie, Margaret Mead, Rosa Parks, and Neil Armstrong courtesy of the Library of Congress. Photographs of Elizabeth Blackwell, Mahatma Gandhi, Albert Einstein, Margaret Bourke-White, Rachel Carson, Mother Teresa, and Jackie Robinson used with permission from AP/Wide World Photos. Photograph of Orville Wright courtesy of the Dayton Metro Library, Wright Brothers Collection. Photograph of Amelia Earhart used with permission from Amy Kleppner (Amelia Earhart™ is a trademark of Amy Kleppner, as heir to the estate of Muriel Morrissey, http://www.AmeliaEarhart .com). Photograph of Marian Anderson used with permission from the Family of James Depreist.

notes

1. Christopher Columbus, *The Log of Christopher Columbus, Selections by Steve Lowe* (New York: Philomel Books, 1992), p. 5.

2. William Least Heat-Moon, *Columbus in the Americas* (Hoboken, NJ: John Wiley and Sons, 2002), pp. 74–76.

3. Diane Stanley, *Leonardo da Vinci* (New York: Morrow Junior Books, 1996), p. 6.

4. Andrew Langley, *Leonardo and His Times* (New York: Dorling Kindersley, 1999), p. 60.

5. Stanley, *Leonardo da Vinci*, p. 16.

6. Kathleen Krull, *Lives of the Artists: Masterpieces, Messes (and What the Neighbors Thought)* (New York: Harcourt, Brace, 1995), p. 12.

7. Kathleen Krull, *Giants of Science: Leonardo da Vinci* (New York: Viking, 2005), p. 73.

8. Vanessa Gera, "Copernicus Reburied as a Hero in Poland," *Boston Globe*, 23 May 2010.

9. Andrea Frova and Mariapiera Marenzana, *Thus Spoke Galileo: The Great Scientist's Ideas and Their Relevance to the Present Day* (New York: Oxford University Press, 2006), p. 122.

10. Kathleen Krull, *Giants of Science: Isaac Newton* (New York: Viking, 2006), pp. 27–28.

11. Ibid., p. 48.

12. Joel Levy, *Newton's Notebook: The Life, Times, and Discoveries of Sir Isaac Newton* (Philadelphia: Running Press, 2009), p. 26.

13. Krull, *Isaac Newton*, p. 10.

14. Elizabeth Cady Stanton, *Eighty Years and More: Reminiscences, 1815–1897* (Amherst, NY: Humanity Books, 2002), p. 12.

15. Ibid., p. 72.

16. Henry David Thoreau, *Walden* (Boston: Beacon Press, 1997), p. 302.

17. Rebecca Hazell, *Heroines: Great Women through the Ages* (New York: Abbeville Publishing Group, 1996), p. 46.

18. George Sullivan, *In Their Own Words: Harriet Tubman* (New York: Scholastic, 2001), p. 44.

19. Kathleen Krull, *Lives of Extraordinary Women: Rulers, Rebels (and What the Neighbors Thought)* (New York: Harcourt, 2000), p. 51.

20. Charles Sumner Young, *Clara Barton: A Centenary Tribute to the World's Greatest Humanitarian* (Boston: Richard G. Badger, 1922), p. 402.

21. Cynthia Klingel and Robert B. Noyed, *Clara Barton: Founder of the American Red Cross* (Chanhassen, MN: Child's World, 2003), p. 28.

22. Barbara Sommervill, *Life Portraits: Elizabeth Blackwell: America's First Female Doctor* (Pleasantville, NY: Gareth Stevens Publishing, 2009), p. 40.

23. Ibid., p. 64.

24. Marc J. Seifer, *Wizard: The Life and Times of Nikola Tesla: Biography of a Genius* (Secaucus, NJ: Carol Publishing Group, 1996), p. 128.

25. Margaret Cheney and Robert Uth, *Tesla: Master of Lightning* (New York: Barnes and Noble Books, 1999), p. 160.

26. Booker T. Washington, *Up from Slavery* (Mattituck, NY: Amereon House, n.d.), p. 18.

27. Ibid., p. 29.

28. Ibid., p. 135.

29. Eve Curie, *Madame Curie: A Biography by Eve Curie* (New York: Doubleday, 1937), pp. 18–21.

30. Mohandas K. Gandhi, *An Autobiography: The Story of My Experiments with Truth*, trans. Mahadev Desai (Boston: Beacon Press, 1993), pp. 50–51.

31. Orville Wright, *How We Invented the Airplane* (New York: David McKay, 1953), p. 8.

32. Kathleen Krull, *Giants of Science: Albert Einstein* (New York: Viking, 2009), p. 18.

33. Jean L. Backus, *Letters from Amelia: 1901–1937* (Boston: Beacon Press, 1982), p. 35.

34. Ibid., p. 66.

35. Rossella Lorenzi, *Discovery News*, June 3, 2010.

36. Susan Ware, *Letter to the World: Seven Women Who Shaped the American Century* (New York: W. W. Norton, 1998), pp. 123–25.

37. Marian Anderson, *My Lord, What a Morning: An Autobiography* (New York: Viking Press, 1956), p. 38.

38. Ibid., pp. 185–88.

39. Margaret Bourke-White, *Portrait of Myself: Margaret Bourke-White* (New York: Simon and Schuster, 1963), pp. 70–71.

40. Martha Freeman, ed., *Always, Rachel: The Letters of Rachel Carson and Dorothy Freeman, 1952–1964* (Boston: Beacon Press, 1995), p. xxiii.

41. Katherine Mangu-Ward, "Suffering in Silence," *Wall Street Journal*, April 20, 2007.

42. Kathryn Spink, *Mother Teresa: A Complete Authorized Biography* (San Francisco: HarperSanFrancisco, 1997), pp. 22–23.

43. Steven Kasher, *The Civil Rights Movement: A Photographic History, 1954–68* (New York: Abbeville Press, 1996), p. 35.

44. Jackie Robinson, *I Never Had It Made*, as told to Alfred Duckett (New York: G. P. Putnam's Sons, 1972), p. 77.

45. Jackie Robinson and Alfred Duckett, *Breakthrough to the Big League: The Story of Jackie Robinson* (New York: Harper and Row, 1965), p. 152.

46. Kathleen Krull, *Lives of the Athletes: Thrills, Spills (and What the Neighbors Thought)* (New York: Harcourt, Brace, 1997), p. 53.

47. Alan Shepard and Deke Slayton, *Moon Shot: The Inside Story of America's Race to the Moon* (Atlanta, GA: Turner, 1994), p. 27.

48. Neil Armstrong, Edwin Aldrin, and Michael Collins, *The*

Notes

First Lunar Landing: As Told by the Astronauts, 20th Anniversary (Washington, DC: NASA, 1989), p. 20.

49. Neil Armstrong, Michael Collins, and Edwin Aldrin, *First on the Moon: A Voyage with Neil Armstrong, Michael Collins, and Edwin E. Aldrin, Jr.*, with Gene Farmer and Dora Jane Hamblin (Boston: Little, Brown, 1970), p. 286.

bibliography

Aaseng, Nathan. *Twentieth-Century Inventors*. New York: Facts on File, 1991.

Adler, David A. *Jackie Robinson: He Was the First*. New York: Holiday House, 1989.

Amper, Thomas. *Booker T. Washington*. Minneapolis: Carolrhoda Books, 1998.

Anderson, Margaret. *Isaac Newton: The Greatest Scientist of All Time*. Springfield, NJ: Enslow, 1996.

Anderson, Marian. *My Lord, What a Morning: An Autobiography*. New York: Viking Press, 1956.

Andronik, Catherine M. *Copernicus: Founder of Modern Astronomy*. Berkeley Heights, NJ: Enslow, 2002.

Armstrong, Neil, Michael Collins, and Edwin Aldrin. *First on The Moon: A Voyage with Neil Armstrong, Michael Collins, and Edwin E. Aldrin, Jr*. Written with Gene Farmer and Dora Jane Hamblin. Boston: Little, Brown, 1970.

———. *The First Lunar Landing: 20th Anniversary, As Told by the Astronauts*. Washington, DC: NASA, 1989.

Atkins, Jeanine. *Girls Who Looked Under Rocks*. Nevada City, CA: Dawn Publications, 2000.

Backus, Jean L. *Letters from Amelia: 1901–1937*. Boston: Beacon Press, 1982.

Baker, Rachel. *The First Woman Doctor*. New York: Scholastic, 1971.

Bibliography

Barker-Benfield, G. J., and Catherine Clinton. *Portraits of American Women: From Settlement to the Present*. New York: Oxford University Press, 1998.

Bartlett, John. *Bartlett's Familiar Quotations*. 16th ed. Edited by Justin Kaplan. New York: Little, Brown, 1992.

Barton, Clara. *The Story of My Childhood*. Charleston, SC: Nabu Press, 2010.

Bateson, Mary Catherine. *With a Daughter's Eye: A Memoir of Margaret Mead and Gregory Bateson*. New York: William Morrow, 1984.

Bloom, Harold, ed. *Henry David Thoreau*. New York and Philadelphia: Chelsea House, 1987.

Bourke-White, Margaret. *Portrait of Myself: Margaret Bourke-White*. New York: Simon and Schuster, 1963.

Brandt, Keith. *Rosa Parks*. [Mahwan, NJ?]: Troll Communications, 1998.

Brenner, Barbara. *If You Were There in 1492*. New York: Aladdin Paperbacks, 1991.

Brown, Don. *One Giant Leap: The Story of Neil Armstrong*. Boston: Houghton Mifflin, 1998.

Burgan, Michael. *Elizabeth Cady Stanton: Social Reformer*. Minneapolis: Compass Point Books, 2006.

Burleigh, Robert. *A Man Named Thoreau*. New York: Atheneum, 1985.

Callahan, Sean. *Margaret Bourke-White: Photographer*. New York: Little, Brown, 1998.

Cheney, Margaret. *Tesla: Man Out of Time*. New York: Simon and Schuster, 1981.

Cheney, Margaret, and Robert Uth. *Tesla: Master of Lightning*. New York: Barnes and Noble Books, 1999.

Cole, Michael D. *Apollo II: First Moon Landing*. Springfield, NJ: Enslow, 1995.

Collier, James Lincoln. *The Clara Barton You Never Knew*. New York: Children's Press, 2003.

Columbus, Christopher. *I, Columbus: My Journal 1492–3*. Edited by Peter and Connie Roop. New York: Walker, 1990.

———. *The Log of Christopher Columbus, Selections by Steve Lowe*. New York: Philomel Books, 1992.

Cullen-DuPont, Kathryn. *Elizabeth Cady Stanton and Women's Liberty.* New York: Facts on File, 1992.

Curie, Eve. *Madame Curie: A Biography by Eve Curie.* New York: Doubleday, 1937.

Demi. *Gandhi.* New York: Margaret K. McElderry Books, 2001.

Derleth, August. *Concord Rebel: A Life of Henry D. Thoreau.* Philadelphia and New York: Chilton, 1962.

Dommermuth-Costa, Carol. *Nikola Tesla: A Spark of Genius.* Minneapolis: Lerner, 1994.

Dyer, Wayne W. *Wisdom of the Ages: A Modern Master Brings Eternal Truths into Everyday Life.* New York: HarperCollins, 1998.

Earhart, Amelia. *The Fun of It: Random Records of My Own Flying and of Women in Aviation.* Chicago: Academy Press, 1977.

Fernandez-Armesto, Felipe. *Columbus.* New York: Oxford University Press, 1991.

Ferris, Helen. *When I Was A Girl: The Stories of Famous Women as Told by Themselves.* New York: MacMillan, 1931.

Ferris, Jeri. *Go Free or Die: A Story about Harriet Tubman.* Minneapolis: Carolrhoda Books, 1988.

Fisher, Leonard Everett. *Galileo.* New York: MacMillan, 1992.

Freeman, Martha, ed. *Always, Rachel: The Letters of Rachel Carson and Dorothy Freeman 1952–1964.* Boston: Beacon Press, 1995.

Fritz, Jean. *You Want Women to Vote, Lizzie Stanton?* New York: G. P. Putnam's Sons, 1995.

Frova, Andrea, and Mariapiera Marenzana. *Thus Spoke Galileo: The Great Scientist's Ideas and Their Relevance to the Present Day.* New York: Oxford University Press, 2006.

Gandhi, Mohandas K. *An Autobiography: The Story of My Experiments with Truth.* Translated by Mahadev Desai. Boston: Beacon Press, 1993.

Glimm, Adele. *Elizabeth Blackwell: First Woman Doctor of Modern Times.* New York: McGraw-Hill, 2000.

Goldberg, Vicki. *Margaret Bourke-White: A Biography.* New York: Harper and Row, 1986.

Greenfield, Eloise. *Rosa Parks.* New York: HarperCollins, 1973.

Bibliography

Hacker, Carlotta. *Women in Profile: Explorers*. New York: Crabtree, 1998.

Hancock, Sibyl. *Famous Firsts of Black Americans*. Gretna, LA: Pelican, 1983.

Haskins, Jim. *One More River to Cross: The Stories of Twelve Black Americans*. New York: Scholastic, 1992.

Hazell, Rebecca. *Heroines: Great Women Through the Ages*. New York: Abbeville Publishing Group, 1996.

Heat-Moon, William Least. *Columbus in the Americas*. Hoboken, NJ: John Wiley and Sons, 2002.

Hitzeroth, Deborah, and Sharon Heerboth. *The Importance of Galileo Galilei*. San Diego, CA: Lucent Books, 1992.

Howard, Jane. *Margaret Mead: A Life*. New York: Simon and Schuster, 1984.

Humphrey, Sandra McLeod. *Dare to Dream! 25 Extraordinary Lives*. Amherst, NY: Prometheus Books, 2005.

Kasher, Steven. *The Civil Rights Movement: A Photographic History, 1954–68*. New York: Abbeville Press, 1996.

Keller, Emily. *Margaret Bourke-White: A Photographer's Life*. Minneapolis: Lerner, 1996.

Kerby, Mona. *Amelia Earhart: Courage in the Sky*. New York: Puffin Books, 1990.

King, David C. *First Facts About American Heroes*. New York: Blackbirch Press, 1996.

Klingel, Cynthia, and Robert B Noyed. *Clara Barton: Founder of The American Red Cross*. Chanhassen, MN: Child's World, 2003.

Kramer, Barbara. *Neil Armstrong: The First Man on the Moon*. Berkeley Heights, NJ: Enslow, 1997.

Krull, Kathleen. *Giants of Science: Albert Einstein*. New York: Viking, 2009.

———. *Giants of Science: Isaac Newton*. New York: Viking, 2006.

———. *Giants of Science: Leonardo da Vinci*. New York: Viking, 2005.

———. *Lives of the Artists: Masterpieces, Messes (and What the Neighbors Thought)*. New York: Harcourt, Brace, 1995.

———. *Lives of the Athletes: Thrills, Spills (and What the Neighbors Thought)*. New York: Harcourt, Brace, 1997.

———. *Lives of Extraordinary Women: Rulers, Rebels (and What the Neighbors Thought)*. New York: Harcourt, 2000.

———. *They Saw the Future: Oracles, Psychics, Scientists, Great Thinkers, and Pretty Good Guessers*. New York: Atheneum Books for Young Readers, 1999.

Langley, Andrew. *Leonardo and His Times*. New York: Dorling Kindersley, 1999.

Lazo, Caroline. *Mahatma Gandhi*. New York: Dillon Press, 1993.

Le Joly, Father Edward, and Jaya Chaliha. *Stories Told by Mother Teresa*. Boston: Element Books, 1999.

Lear, Linda. *Rachel Carson: Witness for Nature*. New York: Henry Holt, 1997.

Levy, Joel. *Newton's Notebook: The Life, Times, and Discoveries of Sir Isaac Newton*. Philadelphia: Running Press, 2009.

MacLeod, Elizabeth. *The Wright Brothers: A Flying Start*. New York: Kids Can Press, 2002.

Manuel, Frank E. *A Portrait of Isaac Newton*. New York: Da Capo Press, 1968.

Martin, Christopher. *Mohandas Gandhi*. Minneapolis: Lerner, 2001.

McClafferty, Carla Killough. *Something Out of Nothing: Marie Curie and Radium*. New York: Farrar Straus Giroux, 2006.

McDonough, Yona Zeldis. *Sisters in Strength: American Women Who Made a Difference*. New York: Henry Holt, 2000.

McGovern, Ann. *"Wanted Dead or Alive": The True Story of Harriet Tubman*. New York: Scholastic, 1965.

McLanathan, Richard. *Leonardo da Vinci*. New York: Harry N. Abrams, 1990.

Mead, Margaret. *Blackberry Winter: My Earlier Years*. Gloucester, MA: Peter Smith Publishers, 1989.

Meltzer, Milton. *Henry David Thoreau: A Biography*. Minneapolis: Twenty-First Century Books, 2007.

Metraux, Rhoda, ed. *Margaret Mead: Some Personal Views*. New York: Walker, 1979.

Montgomery, Mary Ann. *Marie Curie: What Made Them Great Series*. Englewood Cliffs, NJ: Silver Burdett Press, 1990.

Bibliography

Morgan, Nina. *Mother Teresa: Saint of the Poor*. Austin, TX: Raintree Steck-Vaughn Publishers, 1998.

Nicholson, Lois P. *Booker T. Washington*. Philadelphia: Chelsea House, 1997.

Oates, Stephen B. *A Woman of Valor: Clara Barton and the Civil War*. New York: The Free Press, 1994.

Parks, Rosa, with Jim Haskins. *Rosa Parks: My Story*. New York: Puffin Books, 1992.

Parr, Jan. *Amelia Earhart: First Lady of Flight*. New York: Franklin Watts, 1997.

Paston, Amy. *Gandhi*. New York: DK Publishing, 2006.

Perl, Lila. *It Happened in America: True Stories from the Fifty States*. New York: Henry Holt, 1992.

Pflaum, Rosalynd. *Marie Curie and Her Daughter Irene*. Minneapolis: Lerner, 1993.

Reef, Catherine. *Rachel Carson: The Wonder of Nature*. Frederick, MD: Twenty-First Century Books, 1992.

Richardson, Robert D., Jr. *Henry Thoreau: A Life of the Mind*. Berkeley and Los Angeles: University of California Press, 1986.

Robinson, Jackie, and Alfred Duckett. *Breakthrough to the Big League: The Story of Jackie Robinson*. New York: Harper and Row, 1965.

Robinson, Jackie, as told to Alfred Duckett. *I Never Had It Made*. New York: G. P. Putnam's Sons, 1972.

Rosinsky, Natalie M. *Sir Isaac Newton: Brilliant Mathematician and Scientist*. Minneapolis: Compass Point Books, 2008.

Ross, Ishbel. *Child of Destiny: The Life Story of the First Woman Doctor*. New York: Harper and Brothers, 1949.

Ruth, Amy. *Mother Teresa*. Minneapolis: Lerner, 1999.

Sanford, William R., and Carl R. Green. *Jackie Robinson*. New York: Crestwood House, 1992.

Sawyer, Kem Knapp. *Harriet Tubman*. New York: DK Publishing, 2010.

Scott, Richard. *Jackie Robinson*. New York: Chelsea House, 1987.

Schleichert, Elizabeth. *The Life of Elizabeth Blackwell*. Frederick, MD: Twenty-First Century Books, 1992.

Shepard, Alan, and Slayton, Deke. *Moon Shot: The Inside Story of America's Race to the Moon.* Atlanta, GA: Turner, 1994.

Sherrow, Victoria. *Mohandas Gandhi: The Power of the Spirit.* Brookfield, CT: Millbrook Press, 1994.

Shields, Charles J. *Mohandas K. Gandhi.* Philadelphia: Chelsea House, 2002.

Seifer, Marc J. *Wizard: The Life and Times of Nikola Tesla: Biography of a Genius.* Secaucus, NJ: Carol Publishing Group, 1996.

Sommervill, Barbara. *Life Portraits: Elizabeth Blackwell: America's First Female Doctor.* Pleasantville, NY: Gareth Stevens Publishing, 2009.

Spink, Kathryn. *Mother Teresa: A Complete Authorized Biography.* San Francisco: HarperSanFrancisco, 1997.

Stanley, Diane. *Leonardo da Vinci.* New York: Morrow Junior Books, 1996.

Stanton, Elizabeth Cady. *Eighty Years and More: Reminiscences.* Amherst, NY: Humanity Books, 2002.

Steele, Philip. *Galileo: The Genius Who Faced the Inquisition.* Washington, DC: National Geographic, 2005.

———. *Marie Curie: The Woman Who Changed the Course of Science.* Washington, DC: National Geographic, 2006.

Stille, Darlene R. *Extraordinary Women of Medicine.* New York: Children's Press, 1997.

Sullivan, George. *In Their Own Words: Harriet Tubman.* New York: Scholastic, 2001.

Summer, L. S. *Rosa Parks.* [Chanhassen, MN]: Child's World, 2000.

Szabo, Corinne. *Sky Pioneer: A Photobiography of Amelia Earhart.* Washington, DC: National Geographic, 1997.

Tames, Richard. *Mother Teresa.* New York: Franklin Watts, 1989.

Taviani, Paolo Emilio. *Columbus: The Great Adventure.* New York: Orion Books, 1991.

Taylor, M. W. *Harriet Tubman: Antislavery Activist.* Philadelphia: Chelsea House, 1991.

Taylor, Robert. *The First Flight: The Story of the Wright Brothers.* New York: Franklin Watts. 1990.

Teresa, Mother. *No Greater Love.* Novato, CA: New World Library, 1997.

Bibliography

Thoreau, Henry David. *Walden*. Boston: Beacon Press, 1997.

Ulrich, Laurel Thatcher. *Well-Behaved Women Seldom Make History*. New York: Alfred A. Knopf, 2007.

Ventura, Piero. *1492: The Year of the New World*. New York: G. P. Putnam's Sons, 1991.

Vickery, Jim Dale. *Wilderness Visionaries*. Merrillville, IN: ICS Books, 1986.

Ware, Susan. *Letter to the World: Seven Women Who Shaped the American Century*. New York: W. W. Norton, 1998.

Washington, Booker T. *Up from Slavery*. Mattituck, NY: Amereon House, n.d.

Westfall, Richard S. *The Life of Isaac Newton*. New York: Cambridge University Press, 1993.

White, Michael. *Isaac Newton: Discovering Laws That Govern the Universe*. Woodbridge, CT: Blackbirch Press, 1999.

Wolf, Sylvia. *Focus: Five Women Photographers*. Morton Grove, IL: Albert Whitman, 1994.

Wright, Orville. *How We Invented the Airplane*. New York: David McKay, 1953.

Yannuzzi, Della. *New Elements: The Story of Marie Curie*. Greensboro, NC: Morgan Reynolds, 2006.

Young, Charles Sumner. *Clara Barton: A Centenary Tribute to the World's Greatest Humanitarian*. Charleston, SC: Nabu Press, 2010.

Zemlicka, Shannon. *Neil Armstrong*. Minneapolis: Lerner, 2003.